VOICES IN LITERATURE

GOLD

W9-BLC-047

Teacher's Guide

Mary Lou McCloskey

Lydia Stack

Contributing Writer:
Yvette St. John

Heinle & Heinle Publishers
An International Thomson
Publishing Company
Boston, Massachusetts 02116, U.S.A.

ISBN: 0-8384-7033-5
Manufactured in the United States of America.

Heinle & Heinle
An International Thomson Publishing Company
Boston, Massachusetts 02116 U.S.A.

10 9 8 7 6 5 4 3 2

*We would like to thank Angela Gadbois for sharing the "Self
and Peer Evaluation" she developed with her class, and Steve
Rutherford for his ideas on previewing the book.*

*We would also like to acknowledge Jodi Cressman's valuable
contribution to the "Art Notes." Her sharp eye and bright
insights will help students to enjoy and use the fine art
selections as they explore the literature.*

Table of Contents

Introduction

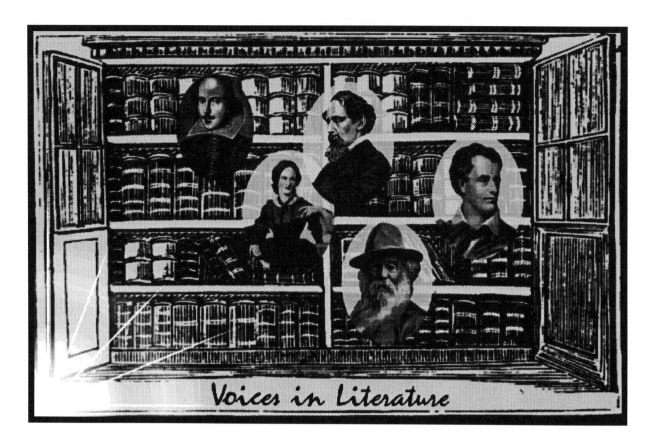

GOALS AND PHILOSOPHY OF *VOICES GOLD*

We have written *Voices in Literature Gold* to provide teachers of English to speakers of other languages (ESOL) and ESOL students with an anthology of high-quality literature. Our goal is to provide both selections and activities that will help students interact with literature to benefit their language learning, to foster literary discussion, and to introduce the language and concepts of literature. We have included a variety of ways for teachers and students to approach the literature selections, to interact with the actual texts, and to respond to the selections.

In this introduction, we address three questions about using literature with learners of English: Why should we use literature with language learners? What literature should we use? How should we teach literature?

Why use literature?

Literature is an appropriate, valuable, and valid medium to help ESOL students and teachers accomplish important goals. Literature provides students with motivation to learn and models of high-quality language while it enhances their imagination, inter-action, and collaboration.

Motivation. Literature motivates students by touching on themes they care about, such as love, fear, changes, and dreams, and by using rich and exciting language. Because good literature is about the human experience, it can affect students across linguistic and cultural barriers.

Models. Although ESOL students are not yet proficient in using English, they are proficient users of another language or languages, have had many academic and non-academic experiences, and are capable of high-level thinking. Language educators must provide appropriate materials for these students, materials that challenge them intellectually without frustrating them linguistically. Carefully chosen literature can provide models of high-quality language, with the sophistication and complexity appropriate to the students' age levels. Literature offers new vocabulary in context and serves as a source for learning about the mechanics of language in authentic settings as they are used by masters of that language.

Imagination.   Imagination is one of the abilities that make us fully human. Literature can give students the means to imagine and think creatively. Literature demands that the reader step into the author's world; good literature demands thought from the reader. Students who are learning a new language need and deserve the challenges to their imaginations which appropriate literature provides.

Interaction and collaboration.   Language is learned best in a setting in which it is put to use. Literature provides a common text from which students can negotiate meaning. Well-selected literature addresses issues that are vital to young readers and that stimulate lively discussion among students. Using literature in combination with collaborative activities helps students understand the literature better, relate it to their own ideas and experiences, and go beyond the literature to produce their own literature-related products.

Learning to interact with and talk about literature.   Our goal is for students to develop an enjoyment of literature and learning that will last a lifetime. In addition, interaction with literature will promote rapid and rich language learning. Developing an interest in literature and language in order to interact with and talk about literature will prepare learners of English to enter grade-level English classes. The chart that follows outlines the literary concepts and terms introduced in *Voices in Literature Gold.*

Literature Concepts and Terms Introduced in *Voices in Literature Gold*			
Unit 1: Style	Unit 2: Suspense	Unit 3: Love	Unit 4: Advice
Simile Irony (3 types) Meter Couplet Ode Rhythm Flashback Character development Theme statement Essay (2 types)	Narrative Poetic license Free verse Folk tales Foreshadowing Anecdotes Point of view (3 types) Synopsis Paraphrase Stanza	Imagery Parallelism Leads and conclusions Metaphor Voice Conflict Contrast Compare and contrast Alliteration Character development	Powerful verbs Rhyme scheme Foot (3 types) Number three in literature Static and dynamic characters Analogy Dialect Proverbs Cliché Idioms Narrative and lyric poems Dialogue

Many of the concepts and terms are introduced more than once. For example, character development is discussed in Unit 1, it is revisited again in Unit 3, and then is expanded upon in Unit 4 through a discussion of static and dynamic characters.

How should we choose literature?

For this text, we have used a broad definition of literature and have included fiction, nonfiction, poetry, and drama. We have selected authentic and rich texts that provide real, high-quality language models. We strongly believe that there is no need to water down the literature used with ESOL students, only to choose it carefully. In choosing selections, we were also guided by the following concerns:

Student interest.   Literature should be age-appropriate and should address themes of interest to the learners. In selections for *Voices Gold,* we have attempted to find characters with whom adolescent learners of English can identify—who come from their own cultures and who are experiencing the conflicts common to their age group and the difficulties of moving from one culture to another.

Linguistic accessibility. The language of the literature should be sufficiently clear and simple for the students to understand, yet also expressive, figurative, and evocative in order to match the maturity and intellectual sophistication of the students. We have included, for example, many poetry selections. Poetry is simple, often using rhyme, rhythm, and repetition to enhance comprehensibility. Yet poetry is also complex, evoking deep emotion and sophisticated thought. We have also included short stories, folk tales, ghost stories, excerpts from plays, and nonfiction articles, all carefully chosen for accessibility to adolescents capable of complex thought, but who are still learning to understand and express those thoughts in English.

Cultural relevance. Literature selected for ESOL students should reflect many cultures, introduce authors from a variety of cultures, address concerns of individuals who are experiencing cultural change, and teach about the new English-speaking culture. The following chart illustrates *Voices'* rich variety of multicultural authors, settings, characters, and themes. For your further reading and reference, we have included at the end of this book a list of resources for teachers on choosing and using literature with adolescent learners of English.

Multicultural Authors, Settings, Characters, and Themes in *Voices Gold* Selections			
Unit 1: Style	Unit 2: Suspense	Unit 3: Love	Unit 4: Advice
• *My moccasins have not walked:* American-Indian author and theme • *Eleven:* Mexican-American author • *We Wear the Mask:* African-American author • *Ode to My Socks:* Chilean author • *The Raiders Jacket:* Mexican-American author and characters	• *The Ghost's Bride:* Chinese-American author and a Chinese setting • *The Wise Woman of Córdoba:* Mexican folktale • *The Hitchhiker:* Korean setting, characters, and author	• *Although I Conquer All the Earth:* authored in India • *Karate:* Vietnamese author and characters • *There Is No Word for Goodbye:* Alaskan-Indian characters and author • *West Side Story:* Polish and Puerto Rican characters	• *Remember:* American-Indian • *A Mother's Advice:* Egyptian folktale • *Mother to Son:* African-American author • *La Peseta* ("The Quarter"): Latino-American author • *Four Directions:* Chinese-American author and characters • *On the Pulse of Morning:* African-American author

Thematic focus. The literary selections for *Voices Gold* were selected and organized thematically. This organization has many advantages for students who are learning English and their teachers. First of all, the themes are chosen for their interest and relevance for multicultural classrooms. Topics are intended to address the questions that are often posed in literature, and which students enjoy addressing: "Why do our personal choices reveal so much about us to the world outside?" "Why do so many cultures have a similar interest in stories of suspense?" "How do different cultures view friendship and love?" "Why do many of the stories we are told try to teach us what is important, honest, and true?" Second, the choice of selections invites student/teacher interaction to make connections. This discussion and debate provides opportunities for related vocabulary and language structures to be used and recycled in a variety of ways. We know that this active use of language in related and varying ways encourages its development and retention. Third, the use of themes provides opportunities for students to actively select and construct their own curriculum, thus increasing their investment in the learning process. Within the selections, in the follow-up activities for each unit, and in additional activities in this guide, teachers, too, have many opportunities to tailor the curriculum for a multicultural, multilevel class.

How can literature be used effectively in the ESOL classroom?

The *Voices in Literature* series incorporates strategies for using literature that allow students to be active participants in the learning process. They make choices about what and how to read and how to respond to that reading. They also become keenly aware of the learning strategies they use. Teachers promote authentic instructional dialogue, use a wide range of cooperative learning strategies, and incorporate a process approach to writing in learning activities.

***Individual and cooperative learning strategies and activities in* Voices Gold.** The following chart summarizes both individual and cooperative learning strategies and activities used in *Voices in Literature Gold*.

Individual and Cooperative Learning Strategies and Activities Used in *Voices in Literature Gold*			
Unit 1: Style	**Unit 2: Suspense**	**Unit 3: Love**	**Unit 4: Advice**
• Ask–Draw–Pair–Share • Summarizing information on chart • Quickwrite • Interview and tally • Cluster Chart • Sunshine Outline • Cause and effect activity • Character development graphic organizer • Interviewing • Outlining with a chart • Compare and contrast activity	• Culture Map • Think–Pair–Share • Character Web • Two-column chart • Venn Diagram • Clustering • Draw the setting • Round Table • Jigsaw • Reader's Theater	• Concentric circles/Using parallel structures • Think–Pair–Share • Story mapping • Marking the poem • Two-column chart • Poetry response form • Quickwrite • Charting words • Ranking Ladder • Venn Diagram • Compare and contrast activity	• Remembering—Four Share • Ranking Ladder • True friends interview • Story mapping • Lessons from childhood • Round Table • Best game debate • Tree of Hope • Advice chart

***Process-writing activities in* Voices Gold.** *Voices in Literature Gold* also incorporates a wide range of process-writing activities to integrate learning to write with learning about literature. The following chart summarizes process-writing activities in the four units of the text.

Process-Writing Strategies and Activities Used in *Voices in Literature Gold*			
Unit 1: Style	**Unit 2: Suspense**	**Unit 3: Love**	**Unit 4: Advice**
• Writing poetry • Writing a memoir • Writing a rhyming couplet • Writing an essay • Writing a news article	• Writing a narrative • Writing in free verse • Writing a folk tale • Writing anecdotes • Writing from another point of view • Writing about poetry	• Writing poetry • Writing with description • Writing and responding to poetry • Writing a personal letter • Writing a comparison	• Writing poetry with repetition • Writing with humor (irony) • Writing about characterization • Writing with analogies • Writing with proverbs • Writing a short story with dialogue

***Use of technology with* Voices Gold.** Because technology can play such an important part in students' school and work experiences, and because a number of you will have access to computers and software in your classrooms or in computer labs, we have included supplementary suggestions for the use of computer applications such as word processing, draw programs, and data base management in conjunction with activities in *Voices*.

***Student and Teacher Empowerment through* Voices.** This text was developed to empower both students and teachers. Students are empowered through their active role in the learning process and the many opportunities they have to choose what they will discuss, read and write about, and how they will carry out those activities. Teachers, too, play very active roles, as they make decisions in using this series. We have provided a wide range of readings, many optional ways to use those readings, and more activities than any class could use in a year. Thus teachers have the power and responsibility to choose and adapt these activities for their classes.

Components of Voices in Literature

Student Text
Voices in Literature student text integrates authentic literature and fine art illustrations with rich, active and interactive classroom learning activities. Learners of English will develop listening, speaking, reading and writing abilities for use in their daily lives and grade-level academic work.

Teacher's Guide
The teacher's guide provides:
- an introduction to the thematic, integrated teaching approach
- a description of several approaches to presenting literature selections
- a guide to the Before you Read and After you Read sections
- classroom strategies for using the activity masters
- detailed teaching suggestions for each activity
- suggestions for extension activities
- notes about the fine art

Activity Masters
The reproducible activity masters include forms for activities included in the book and for additional activities, as well as checklists for students and teachers. Many of them are graphic organizers that can be used to enliven classroom contexts beyond those introduced in the text. Al of them encourage high-level thinking and open-ended responses. These versatile materials can be used with *Voices* and other materials.

Audiocassette
Recordings of selected poetry, short stories, and non-fiction provide powerful and memorable language input, including some author's recordings of their own work. Students can listen to the cassette before reading to understand the mood or feeling of a piece. They can listen to the recordings again after reading to reinforce language comprehension of the selection. The recordings capture the rhythm, rhyme and movement of English.

Journal
The Journals provide additional practice in writing, drawing, painting and in the higher order thinking skills introduced in each of the thematic units of *Voices*. These highly creative Journal activities can be used in class or assigned as homework.

Assessment

The Assessment provides teachers with a variety of assessment opportunities that accommodate various levels of English learners. The components include:

- a portfolio assessment system including forms for student, teacher and parent evaluation and response
- end of unit assessment
- personal journal assessment
- scoring guides
- checklists to record student growth

The Teacher's Guide to the Heinle & Heinle ESL Program

The Heinle & Heinle ESL program consists of the two series: *Making Connections 1, 2, and 3* and *Voices in Literature Bronze, Silver, and Gold*, which can be used independently or together. The Teacher's Guide to the Heinle & heinle ESL Program provides much practical advice and strategies for using the two series together. In this guide, classroom practitioners will learn how to take advantage of the revisitation of terms, themes, content and literature in *Making Connections* and *Voices in Literature*. Because the language, content, and literature are organized thematically, students can continuously relate and analyze academic concepts and literary works. This Teacher's Guide also offers strategies for providing instruction to students at many levels—from beginning English language proficiency to advanced levels of content-based and literature-based instruction. A technology section describes how instructors can use electronic support, such as e-mail and software, to expand on the activities found in *Making Connections* and *Voices in Literature*.

FEATURES OF
VOICES GOLD

How is* Voices Gold *structured? We have used a variety of strategies and structures to support students as they learn language through literature and literature through language. The literature is organized thematically, so that students are given opportunities to relate concepts and literary works to one another. The revisitation of themes, ideas, and terms enhances contextual information and thus improves comprehensibility. The supportive activities follow an "into-through-beyond" model that includes activities for before, during, and after reading the literature.

Additional support materials can be found in the appendices that have been added to this level of the series.

Features for each selection:

Fine Art

The selections in *Voices in Literature Gold* are illustrated with full-color fine art prints and photographs selected for their quality, their connections to the literature, their appeal to young readers, and their ability to evoke thoughts and feelings from students. We urge you to take advantage of this lovely "art gallery" by encouraging your students to talk about the art as well as the literature, and to look for connections between the two. In the teacher notes for each selection, we have often provided background information about the artists and have suggested questions that encourage discussion about the illustrations and relate fine art to literature.

Before You Read

Two sections precede each selection to guide students "into" the work. *Exploring Your Own Experience* helps students to investigate concepts and themes that will appear in the literature as they occur in their own lives. *Background* provides contextual information that will make the work more comprehensible and more interesting to students.

The Selection

We encourage you to use a variety of ways to guide students "through" the reading. To accommodate the varied levels of students, you might choose one or a combination of these strategies for using the literature: read aloud, shared reading, choral reading, jigsaw, silent reading, independent reading outside class, or reading and discussing a portion of the selection at a time. Our selections are authentic—they are reproduced exactly as the authors wrote them—but occasionally we have extracted selections from longer works. Longer pieces are also often divided into sections to make them more accessible to your language learners. After each work, we have included information *About the Author* for you and your students to read and discuss. We want students to see the writing process as something they can do, and we want them to see authors as real people. We also have chosen authors who are interesting to students and whose lives show our linguistically and culturally diverse classes of students that they, too, can grow up to be successful—at writing or at something else they choose.

After You Read

After each selection there are several activities that help students go "beyond" to learn from the literature. *What Do You Think?* offers questions that give students genuine opportunities to explore their ideas about the literature and that require them to return to the literature to document and defend those ideas. These are not "display" questions that merely test comprehension; rather they are thought-provoking queries with no one right answer that encourage higher-level thinking skills on the part of students. *Try This* includes activities that incorporate learning strategies and cooperative learning activities to develop concepts related to the literature. *Learning About Literature* provides descriptions, definitions, and activities designed to expand and build on comprehension of literary concepts and terms used in and with the selection. *Writing* applies a process approach to writing; it offers students opportunities to select topics and experiment with writing activities using themes and forms inspired by the literature. We have included activities at all stages of the writing process in *Voices Gold,* including prewriting, drafting (often in the form of journal activities), responding to one another's writing, revising, editing, and publishing.

Unit Follow-Up

At the end of each unit, we have included *Unit Project Ideas,* activities to help students relate the works to one another around the unit theme as well as review and explore further concepts developed in the unit. Also following each unit is a *Further Reading* list for students. The list often includes the sources of selections so that students who become interested in a particular author or work can read further. We also encourage you and your students to expand the list with related literature that interests the class. The Activity Masters (discussed below) include a page with *Further Reading* suggestions for each unit. Each page has additional space for you and your students to add your own choices. We would very much appreciate your sharing these lists with us so we can pass them on to others using the book.

Activity Masters

Reproducible *Activity Masters* are available for *Voices in Literature Gold.* These masters include forms for activities included in the book and for additional activities, as well as checklists for students and teachers. Many of them are graphic organizers that can be used to enliven classroom contexts besides those introduced in the text. All of them encourage high-level thinking and open-ended responses. Many encourage student interaction and cooperation as well.

Special text features:

Appendix A

"The Raven" by Edgar Allen Poe and *Romeo and Juliet,* act II, scene 2, by William Shakespeare are two of the longer, more difficult selections found in *Voices Gold.* Because these selections may be more challenging, they are not presented in their entirety in their respective units. Appendix A contains the remaining lines from the two selections. The individual instructor can decide if there is enough time to read the entire literary selection. If an instructor feels that the text is going to prove too difficult, a good stopping place has been provided in the unit, which still allows the students a measure of completion. All the pre- and post-exercises for "The Raven" and *Romeo and Juliet* can be used whether the selections are read in their entirety or not. Instructors and students may decide that extra credit is appropriate for finishing the readings in the appendix.

Appendix B

Appendix B is a *Guide to Literary Terms and Techniques.* The terms described under *Learning About Literature* after each selection have been pulled out, alphabetized, and defined in this appendix. The majority of the entries contain a page reference so students and teachers can turn to the page and see the definition again in context. Many of the literary terms in *Voices Gold* are recycled after they are first introduced. When the terms are recycled they are italicized in the text. If the students have difficulty remembering a term from a previous selection or unit when they see the italicized word(s), they can turn to Appendix B for the definition.

Appendix C

Appendix C contains the words footnoted in the literary selections throughout the book in alphabetical order. This *Glossary* serves as a quick reference for students and instructors.

INSTRUCTIONAL MANAGEMENT FOR *VOICES GOLD*

Class composition

ESL programs can be composed in many ways: some of you may use *Voices Gold* for multileveled ESL literature classes; some of you may use the text as a component of an ESL language program; some of you may use it as an alternate text for ESL students in mainstream classrooms. To meet all these varied situations, flexibility has been a key word in the development of the *Voices* series. The texts can fit into ESL programs in many ways. We have tried to provide each unit with more activities than you probably will need, in order to give you choices as you determine what is most appropriate for your students. You also have the option of skipping selections altogether, or teaching selections or entire units in a different sequence from that in the book. You can use the Activity Masters to tailor the text to your class, helping students to find activities that are appropriately challenging, but not frustrating.

Time

Voices can also be used flexibly over time. You might choose to use it as a text for a literature course taught daily. Depending on the length of your class period and the levels of your students, each unit may take from two to four weeks to complete. *Voices* can also be used as the literature component for your ESOL language program in which the units might take even longer to cover. Or you may use *Voices* to provide alternate readings for students in a grade-level English class. In any of these situations, you will choose those selections and activities that are relevant and at an appropriate level of difficulty for your students.

Assessment and evaluation

The approach of *Voices Gold* encourages:

- active roles for students
- authentic activities that are meaningful and motivating to students
- interaction and collaboration in pairs, small groups, and class group

- development of language for and through literary discourse
- choices among "into-through-beyond" activities that accommodate students' varying language levels and educational backgrounds

Evaluation should encourage opportunities to:

- evaluate the learning process, not just the end product
- compare students primarily with themselves, rather than with others
- evaluate students as individuals and as parts of teams
- have students evaluate themselves along with the teacher's evaluation
- evaluate students' learning based on multiple, not unitary, measures

Many of the activities in the text lend themselves easily to this kind of evaluation. We have included suggestions for assessment opportunities that occur in each unit in the Teacher Notes chapter of this guide.

We also encourage you to try one or more of the following learning/assessment processes.

Contract

A contract helps students take responsibility for their grades as evaluations that they choose and earn, not that teachers give them. Use a contract with students with each unit, or for each term. In the contract, specify clearly what students must do to achieve a grade of A, B, C, or whatever. You can easily incorporate choice activities and group activities, and can even require in the contract that some activities and projects get your approval. This will help you make sure that activities are at appropriate levels for students. A sample contract follows.

Sample Contract for Unit 1, *Voices in Literature Gold*

To receive an "A" for this unit, in addition to meeting the "B" requirements:

_____ Take a second piece of writing through all the stages of the writing process or complete a second unit project.

To receive a "B" for this unit, in addition to meeting the "C" requirements:

_____ Take one writing selection through all the stages of the writing process (prewriting, drafting, peer discussion, revision, teacher conference, editing, publishing).

_____ Take leadership roles in small group activities in class.

To receive a "C" for this unit, in addition to meeting the "D" requirements:

_____ Keep a literary journal; make an entry for each selection covered.

_____ After approval of choice and procedures, complete one unit project to the standards agreed on with the teacher.

To receive a "D" for this unit:

_____ Attend 90% of classes.

_____ Participate in all class and group activities on the literature.

_____ Draft at least four pieces of writing and discuss two with a peer response group.

Portfolios

You can help students to develop portfolios of their work throughout the term or year. Portfolios can provide documentation for students' development in using language and understanding literature. Portfolios are not just random selections of student work samples, but are collections comprising work that is systematically selected and evaluated according to set criteria. The portfolio might include checklists, journals or logs, contracts, surveys, tests, quizzes, story retelling, teacher notes and observations, and other forms of information. Further readings on portfolios are included in the bibliography at the back of this Teacher's Guide.

Literary Journal

As your students read *Voices Gold,* have them keep their responses to the literature in literary journals. They can note the dates on which they read the selections in *Voices* and outside reading as well. If you choose, you can make the journals interactive by responding to students' writings in the journals or on self-stick notes on the pages. Suggestions for journal assignments are included in several of the units in *Voices Gold.* Further readings on journals for ESOL are included in the bibliography in the back of this Teacher's Guide.

Checklists

A number of checklists are included in the Activity Masters for *Voices Gold,* including the **Group Project Evaluation** chart **(Activity Master #15),** the **Ways of Speaking English** chart **(Activity Master #37),** the **Conferring and Responding to Writing** chart **(Activity Master #6),** the **Writing Process** chart **(Activity Master #13),** and the **Editing Checklist (Activity Master #14).** These can be used for both teacher assessment and student self-assessment. We suggest that you have students staple the Conferring and Responding to Writing Chart and the Editing Checklist to the back cover of their writing folders and the Writing Process Chart to the front cover. As you introduce the skills and concepts on the charts, have students highlight them. Students will know that they are responsible for those aspects of writing when they make revisions and edit. You will know, even for students who enter during the year, which aspects have been taught to students and what you can expect of them.

Four additional checklists, which you may use with *Voices Gold,* are included in the Appendix to this Teacher's Guide. These include an Oral/Aural Language Checklist, a Reading Checklist, a Writing Checklist, and a Student Self-Assessment Form. You can schedule the use of any or all of these instruments periodically during the school year (perhaps at the end of each unit, once during each term, or at the beginning and end of each course) to assess student progress and achievements.

We hope that you and your students enjoy using the selections and activities in *Voices Gold* and that they enrich your classroom learning community. We encourage you to write and share with us your experiences with *Voices Gold.*

TEACHER NOTES

UNIT 1: STYLE

Art Notes

Cover: "Man and Woman," by Rufino Tamayo, 1981

Background:

Rufino Tamayo (1899-1991) was born in Oaxaca, Mexico. He studied painting in the San Carlos Academy in Mexico City. He combined native folk themes with modern European forms such as cubism.

Discussion suggestions:

Note: The questions and ideas for discussion in the Art Notes and throughout the Teacher's Guide are intentionally written at a wide range of difficulty levels so that you will be free to select from them and adapt them to the proficiencies, levels, and interests of your students.

1. Have students describe the painting. Is it simple or complex? Do the figures look real or not?
2. Have students suggest ways that the painting illustrates the idea of "Voices in Literature."
3. Tell students that the title of the painting is "Man and Woman." Ask them if knowing the title makes them think any differently about the painting. Point out the opposition and symmetry that structures the painting. (In each figure, one arm is red, the other blue; one's torso is blue, the other's is red; the red border frames the two brown arches.) Then ask students to relate this structure to the painting's title.
4. Have students compare this painting to an earlier painting by Tamayo (p. 206). Each painting depicts a human figure. Ask students to describe differences between the paintings.
5. Have students guess what the red band with gold knobs might represent. Why is it on the woman's side?

Previewing the Book

To facilitate students' understanding and appreciation of *Voices Gold,* have them preview the book before reading. This will increase the students' comfort level in approaching the book as well as assist them in learning the vocabulary necessary for talking or writing about books.

First, ask students to spend a few minutes looking through the book. After about five minutes, give students the following questions on an overhead or in a handout. Have students work in pairs filling out questions 1-5, then individually work on questions 6-9, and later share with a partner. Finally, ask volunteers to share what unit, art, and photographs they chose with the whole class.

1. Is the *Table of Contents* in the front or back of the book? What is a Table of Contents? Check other books to see where the Table of Contents is.

2. Find the *Glossary.* Is it in the front or back of the book? How will you use it?

3. Find the *Guide to Literary Terms and Techniques.* Is it in the front or back of the book? How could it be useful?

4. The publisher and copyright date are used when listing books in a bibliography. Is this information for *Voices in Literature* in the front or back of the book? Who is the publisher, and what is the copyright date of this book?

5. Give the title for each of the four units:

    1. _____

    2. _____

    3. _____

    4. _____

6. Which unit is the most interesting to you? What interests you about the unit? Do the titles of the selections in the unit fit in with the title of the unit in your opinion?

7. *Voices* has a lot of art work. Find one piece that you like. Why did you choose this one?

8. *Voices* also has many photographs. Find one that you like and tell what you see in the photograph.

9. Share what you have discovered about the book with your partner.

Follow the preview with a general discussion about literature. Ask students to respond to the following in their journals: "What does literature mean to you? Make a list of questions (things you want to learn) about literature." Ask students to be aware of their questions, and to see if they can answer them as you progress through the term.

Technology Note: Students can keep electronic journals, and you can respond to them electronically by using a word processor or by sending "journal-type" messages using messaging software or e-mail.

Student Edition pp. 2–3

Art Notes

Unit Opener: "Walk on the Bridge," by August Macke, 1912

Background:

August Macke (1887-1914) was born in Westphalia, Germany, and later studied in Cologne and Bonn. He joined a group of artists known as "Blue Rider" (named after a painting by Marc of a blue horse and Kandinsky's riders dressed in blue). The blue riders were known for their bold use of color, expression of emotion, and disruption of conventional form. Macke was killed in the trenches during the First World War.

Discussion suggestions:

1. Discuss the meaning of "style." Ask students how the painting illustrates "style."
2. Have students describe the "style" of the painting. Is it colorful or bland? Detailed or simple? Flat-looking or deep-looking? Realistic or abstract?
3. Ask students to find other paintings in this style in *Voices Gold.* (They may point to Matisse's shared use of flat figures and color [pp. 12, 184] or to Oskar Schlemmer's similar simplification of the human figure [p. 40].)

Before You Read   Student Edition p. 4

Activity Master 1

ACTIVITY MASTER #1

Use with student text page 4.

Family Interview

Directions:
Ask an older family or community member these questions. Use another language if you like. Write down the answers and/or draw pictures of the answers.

1. What clothing did you wear when you were my age? *I wore a buba and a wrappa.*
2. Where did you live then? *Bida, Nigeria*
3. What did your parents do to make a living? *My father was a driver for the Ministry of Works. My mother sold onions and peppers in the market.*
4. What clothing did your parents wear when they were my age? *My mother wore a buba and a wrappa. My father wore pants and a shirt or a riga for special occasions.*
5. Where did your parents live then? *Doko, Nigeria*
6. How did their parents make a living? *They were farmers.*

Exploring Your Own Experience: Ask–Draw–Pair–Share.   Ask-Draw-Pair-Share is a four-step process.

1. **Ask:** Students should become familiar with the interview questions. Have them write the questions leaving space to either record a description or state how they are using drawings or photos. Some students may not be living with parents. Suggest alternative persons to interview—older persons from their culture who are

either friends, paraprofessionals, or teachers in the school. Students should have a clear idea of whom to interview before beginning the assignment.

2. **Draw:** Have students record the information and illustrate with drawings or photos.

3. **Pair:** Have students share the information with a partner.

4. **Share:** Place two pairs of students together to make a foursome. Ask each student to share his or her partner's information with the other pair. After having the opportunity to work in the group of four, some students may wish to share the information with the whole class. An advantage of *pair-share* is the rehearsal time that students have before facing the whole class.

Drawings, photos, and explanations can be posted on a bulletin board creating cultural and generational images. Before reading the selection, use the art on p. 6 to discuss the vocabulary of the poem with students. Help students become familiar with "feather" and "headdress."

Student Edition p. 6

Art Notes

"Portrait of an Indian Man," by Jack Hokeah

Background:

Jack Hokeah was born on the Kiowa reservation in Oklahoma in 1902. He studied art both at the University of Oklahoma and the Santa Fe Indian School in New Mexico. This portrait stands out from other Kiowa paintings, which usually show the full figure.

Discussion suggestions:

1. Ask students how the painting illustrates the poem. Does the painting represent the speaker of the poem or something else in the poem?
2. A portrait is usually thought of as a pictorial representation of a particular person. Ask students to identify the elements of this painting that make this figure an "individual." (Students may point to the man's feathers, his beadwork, his face paint, his hair jewelry.)
3. Ask students to describe the figure's facial expression. What might the figure be thinking?

After You Read

Student Edition p. 8

What Do You Think? In this section and throughout *Voices,* we have attempted to ask questions that have no clear "right" answer, but which require students to go back to the text and find passages that support an idea. There are a variety of ways to use the questions in the *What Do You Think?* section. Here are some suggestions from which to choose to fit the needs of your class.

• **Whole Group Work:** Have the class discuss the questions as a group. In order to facilitate student interchange, have students call on each other rather than redirecting the attention back to you, the teacher, after each response. When a student finishes responding to the question you have asked, he or she can call on the next person (hand raised) wishing to contribute to the discussion. The student called on can respond to the original question, respond to what other students have said, or ask for clarification. You can judge when it is time to stop the discussion of one question and move on to the next.

• **Pair Work:** Have pairs of students work on the questions, producing one product. They can take turns writing the answers to the questions or discuss the questions orally in preparation for whole-class discussion. How you choose the partners depends on your purpose. If you want students to practice English, you might assign partners from different language groups. If you want students to become comfortable working with pairs or in groups, you might let students choose their own partners or pair students who have the same native language. Working in pairs is an excellent way to begin cooperative learning.

- **Small Group Work:** Have students answer questions in small cooperative groups. Appointing students to function in the group with specific roles will help this process. For example, one student can record, another read the questions aloud, and another encourage participants, or check the text for examples.

- **Jigsaw:** Jigsaws can be used in several ways.

  1. *Cooperative Group Jigsaw:* Have cooperative groups work on the questions. Each person in the group is responsible for answering one or two questions. Ask students to formulate answers, then share the answers with the rest of the group. If the questions are extremely challenging, "expert" groups can be formed. Students working on question 3, for example, would get together with other students working on this question and formulate answers. Then each student would go back to his or her base group and share what they discussed in the "expert" group.

  2. *Whole-Class Jigsaw:* Assign groups or pairs of students one question so that each group has a different question. Then have students share their thoughts about the question with the whole class.

  3. *One-Question Jigsaw:* Ask students to "jigsaw" parts of a question. For example, question 1 in this section asks students to retell the poem. If this is too large a chunk for individual students to handle, ask pairs or groups to work on one stanza or a group of lines. Then have students sequentially share the retelling of the poem, which could also include illustrations to facilitate comprehension.

- **Homework:** After the class discusses the questions, assign these as written homework. If you want more preparation before class discussion, assign the questions as homework ahead of time.

Hint: To break the routine of working only from the book and give students a change of focus, put the questions on the chalkboard or overhead. Remind students that they still need to use the text to support answers.

Activity Master 2

Try This: Summarizing Information on a Chart. Your students' charts will vary from the following sample.

Use with student text page 8.

Styles of Generations

	What clothing did they wear?	Where did they live?	How did they make a living?
My family	dresses pants skirts shirts blouses suits	California	accountant
My parents' families when my parents were young	buba pants wrappa shirts riga	Bida, Nigeria	driver
My grandparents' families when my grandparents were young	buba pants wrappa shirts riga	Doko, Nigeria	farmers

Extension 1: Walking Gallery. Have students create individual charts on large pieces of paper, which can then be posted around the room and toured by students as in a gallery. During the tour, have students take notes on what they find interesting in other students' charts or use self-stick notes to post their responses.

Extension 2: Cooperative Charts. If you have several students from different language groups, you may wish to have them create charts for their language group as cooperative projects.

Student Edition p. 9

Learning About Literature: Repetition. Have students memorize the poem. If students feel this would be difficult, point out that poems with repetition are easier to memorize. You can "jigsaw" the memorization, having each student memorize a line or two, then recite their lines in sequence.

Before You Read   **Student Edition p. 10**

Exploring Your Own Experience: Do a Quickwrite.   This topic may be challenging for some students. To help them, it is important to begin by sharing your own embarrassing experience. After telling the class your story, use the overhead and begin to write your story, modeling the quickwrite technique. Tell students if they can think of nothing to write, they should write, "I can't think of anything," over and over until an idea comes into their mind. During a quickwrite, pens should not stop moving. Some students may need more share time before they try to write. Others may need freedom to choose another topic.

Technology Note: Quickwrites can be done with a word processor. Turn the monitor off or the brightness down so the screen is blank. This will help students focus on their thoughts rather than the correctness of their writing.

Student Edition pp. 11–15

Reading the Story: With the *Voices Gold* selections, you may wish to vary your approach to proceeding "through" the pieces depending on reading difficulty and length. The following are some alternate ways of reading the literature selections.

1. **Shared Reading:**   Have the class work together on the same text at the same time.

    a) Read aloud while the class follows the text from the book or on an overhead.
    b) Have students read by turns.
    c) Have students read when called upon by you or by another student.

2. **Paired Reading:**   Ask students to read aloud in pairs, alternating paragraphs or logical sections.

3. **Jigsaw:**   Have pairs or groups of students read an assigned section, with each pair or group having a different section. Then ask pairs or groups to share what they have read with the whole class.

4. **Silent Reading:**   Have students read a piece silently in the classroom and then respond in their journal to their reading.

5. **Chunking:**   Ask students to read not read straight through, but in logical "chunks." After each "chunk," have students discuss or respond to it in a journal. Chunking can be silent or oral, or you can alternate oral "chunks" with silent "chunks."

Student Edition p. 12

Art Notes   "The Reader," by Henri Matisse, 1906

Background: Henri Matisse (1869-1954) began life as a law clerk. After a bout with appendicitis, he became intrigued with painting and soon abandoned the law to study art in Paris. He was known across Europe and the United States for his bold innovations in expressive color and decorative pattern. Unlike many expressionists, he was very popular during his lifetime, especially with young people.

Discussion suggestions:
1. Ask students to describe the expression on the figure's face. What is she thinking? Is there a sentence or phrase in the story that describes her expression?
2. Have students compare this painting to Matisse's earlier work (p. 100) and later work (p. 184). What do the paintings have in common? How are they different? Do students see a trend or pattern of development in Matisse's work?

After You Read   **Student Edition p. 16**

Activity Master 3

Try This: Description by Comparison. Discuss with the students some common similes, for example, "The clouds are like marshmallows." Instruct students to fill in **Activity Master #3 (Food Similes).** You might wish to have students work in pairs to help generate ideas for the chart. Students' answers will vary from the following sample.

ACTIVITY MASTER #3

Use with student text page 16.

Food Similes

Food:	Broccoli	Potatoes	Parsley	Mushrooms	Grapes
Reminds me of:	fallen trees	people watching TV	lace	umbrellas	marbles
	people resting	farmer's suntanned skin	trees	people wearing hats	many eyes
	clubs	dirty knees	clouds	tents	balls
	giant's legs				crowded room

For questions 1 and 2 on p. 17, assign pairs or groups of students a page of the story from which to find similes.

Note: No words are glossed in the selection. Ask students if they feel this is appropriate for their ease in understanding. Would they have glossed some words? Which ones?

Supplementary Activity: Round Table

1. Cut out pictures or portions of pictures from magazines and glue them on index cards. The pictures should be ones that will evoke similes, such as:

Picture	Simile
clouds	ships
spaghetti	traffic intersection
grass	haircut
cauliflower	crowd of white-haired people from above

2. Give each student a card.
3. Have students get into groups of three or four.
4. Instruct each student to hold up his or her card for the group to see. The group will then orally give as many similes as they can. Assign a student to be a timer and allow two minutes for each card.
5. Give individual students paper.
6. Instruct students to staple or clip the card to the top of the paper and write as many similes as they can under the picture. Remind students that the group's sharing should stimulate their thinking.
7. Post all the papers and allow students time to view each other's work.

Student Edition p. 17

Activity Master 4

Writing: A Childhood Memoir. Model for the students your "ages" using a wooden stacking doll or drawing of "onion" rings. If you have a stacking doll, take apart the doll and give each an "age." Choose the age you will be and tell the story associated with that age to the students. Modeling is very important to help students understand what is expected of them. Discuss the use of "eleven-year-old words."

Following is an example of an onion with the ages inside:

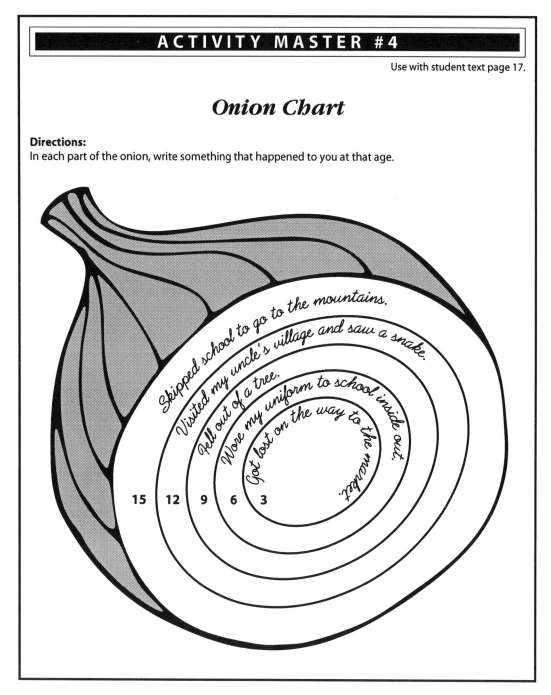

ACTIVITY MASTER #4

Onion Chart

Directions:
In each part of the onion, write something that happened to you at that age.

Skipped school to go to the mountains.

Visited my uncle's village and saw a snake.

Fell out of a tree.

Wore my uniform to school inside out.

Got lost on the way to the market.

15   12   9   6   3

Note: When students write their stories, their six- or ten-year-old selves may speak only the language of their country of birth. They may find it easier to use words from their native languages.

▼ We Wear the Mask, by Paul Laurence Dunbar

Before You Read   **Student Edition p. 18**

Activity Master 5

Exploring Your Own Experience: Masks.   Begin this activity by telling an experience of your own and/or one from literature that the class has shared. In order to assist students in brainstorming a situation in which they felt like crying but smiled instead, you might try the following:

1. Ask students to think of situations in which they had to put on a happy face and make a list of those times. You can model by making your own list on the chalkboard or overhead.
2. Ask students to choose the situation that they want to talk about and circle it on their list.

Because the act of writing promotes thinking, brainstorming helps students who become "stuck," or can think of nothing to talk about. The list also gives students a choice about what they want to share. We have included a sample completed **Activity Master #5 (Masks)**. Your students may produce even more creative illustrations.

ACTIVITY MASTER #5

Use with student text page 18.

Masks

Directions:
For many different reasons, people sometimes choose to hide their real feelings. In "Eleven," Rachel was upset because she couldn't hide her feelings, but instead cried in front of everyone. Have you ever been in a situation where you felt like crying but instead smiled, or where you felt angry but instead put on a calm face?

1. Think about the situation.
2. Discuss your experience with a small group of classmates.
3. Draw two masks to show the way you felt and the face you showed.
4. You may choose to share your masks with the class and/or put them in a class display.

MY MASKS
A brief description of the situation: *I just started a new school. I wanted to make friends. But at recess they laughed at the way I pronounced some words.*

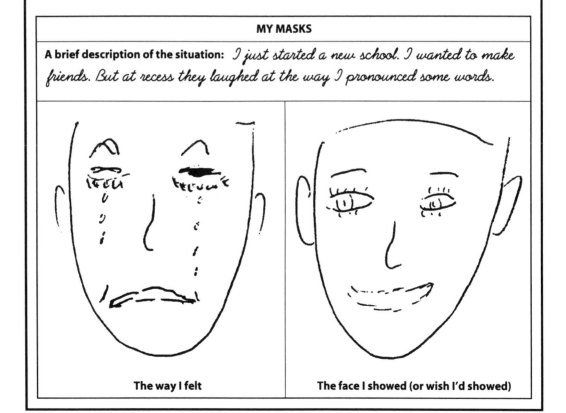

| The way I felt | The face I showed (or wish I'd showed) |

Note: To promote intercultural communication, use this opportunity to discuss the similarities and differences in revealing feelings for the cultures represented in your classroom. Which feelings do students consider appropriate to show? Which do they prefer to hide? Are there individual and cultural differences? Similarities?

Background: The vocabulary in the poem is challenging. Try the following suggestions to help students enjoy and understand the language of the poem.

1. Rendering the Poem:

a) Instruct students to mark words or phrases they like as you read the poem aloud a few times. These can be chosen because students like the meaning or just the sound of the words. Have students mark copies of the poem or use self-stick notes.

b) Ask students to read the words or phrases they have marked at random or in turn. Repeating what someone else has read is fine. Do this with no discussion between students' readings.

Rendering allows students to savor and enjoy the language of the poem before the "work" of analysis begins. Also, students realize they have a general understanding of what the poem is about even if they don't understand all the words. Be sure to point out to them how much they *do* understand before focusing on what they don't.

2. Chart the Meaning:

a) Ask students to choose two or three words they want to understand better and write the words and their meanings.

b) Elicit the words from students and make a class chart of "Student-Chosen Words" and their meanings.

c) Ask students to choose a word or phrase from the chart. This could be done in pairs.

d) Tell students to draw a picture that illustrates the meaning of the word or phrase.

e) Post the results.

3. Strategies: Students need to be aware of a variety of strategies for dealing with new words.

a) Look up the words and include them in a personal dictionary.

b) Ask another student or the teacher what the words mean.

c) Try to get the meaning from context.

d) Write the words in a notebook and look them up at a later time.

Technology Note: Students can add new words and definitions to their personal dictionaries on a word processor, then use the Line- or Paragraph-Sort feature to alphabetize the file and print it for inclusion in their notebooks. Once they are confident that they know words well, they can delete them from the file.

Student Edition p. 20

Art Notes

"Les Fetiches," by Lois Mailou Jones, 1938

Background:

Lois Mailou Jones was born in Boston, where she began studying art at age fourteen. She later attended the Museum School of Fine Arts. Because of racial discrimination, she was denied a teaching position at the school. She worked as a textile designer, taught at Howard University in Washington, D.C., and then went to study in Paris.

Discussion suggestions:

1. Ask students to discuss ways that the painting illustrates the poem. Ask them to find particular lines in the poem that apply to the painting.

2. Ask students what emotions the painting brings out for them.

3. Ask students if each mask shows different emotions. Which mask would they wear if they were angry? Sad? Scared? Surprised?

4. Point out how each mask conveys symmetry (so that if you divide the mask in half, each half matches the other almost exactly). Then ask students what the lines around the top mask do to the painting (suggest motion?). The symmetry, along with the flat colors gives each mask a simple quality; but all the masks together give the entire painting a sense of motion.

5. Have students guess what the orange figure on the right side of the painting represents.

After You Read

Student edition p. 22

What Do You Think? You may wish to provide students with more background information on slavery, civil rights, and racism to help them better understand the world that Dunbar faced.

Learning About Literature: Meter. You can illustrate meter by putting a few lines of the poem on the chalkboard or overhead and marking the meter. Here is an example of a line with meter marked:

> ⌣ ´ ⌣ ´ ⌣ ´ ⌣ ´
> *We wear the mask that grins and lies,*
> ⌣ ´ ⌣ ´ ⌣ ´ ⌣ ´
> *It hides our cheeks and shades our eyes—*

"Jigsaw" the poem by asking pairs of students to mark sets of lines. Discuss the regular metered pattern in the poem.

Extension 1: Marking Meter. Ask pairs of students to think of a song they know, write out a few lines, and mark it for meter. Some students may wish to try marking meter on a few lines of a song or poetry written in their native language.

Extension 2: Rhyming Couplets. Demonstrate rhyming couplets with another poem or song that many of the students know. If your school has a school song, it may contain couplets. The United States' national anthem has rhyming couplets.

Student Edition p. 23

Try This: Finding the Rhyme. The rhyme scheme for the poem is as follows:

1st Stanza		2nd Stanza		3rd Stanza	
lies	a	*otherwise*	a	*cries*	a
eyes	a	*sighs*	a	*arise*	a
guile	b	*while*	b	*vile*	b
smile	b	*mask*	c	*mile*	b
subtleties	a			*otherwise*	a
				mask	c

Student Edition p. 23

Activity Master 6

Writing: Rhyming Couplets

- **Imaging:** You may wish to play relaxing music while students close their eyes to picture what they would like to write about. Many classical music selections work well, such as Pachelbel's "Canon in C" or one of your favorites. Encourage students to choose another topic if they do not wish to write about a time they wore a mask.

- **Group Work:** When students have selected a topic, ask them to draft a line or two. Target key words and have the group suggest related rhyming words.

- **Feedback:** **Activity Master #6 (Conferring and Responding to Writing)** is designed to be used for student response groups. You may wish to adapt these charts, taking into consideration the nature of the writing task and the previous experience students have had with responding in peer groups.

If your students need practice, use **Activity Master #6** as follows to assist them in becoming skilled at giving encouraging feedback.

1. Hand out copies of the response chart to the response groups. Give each student enough charts to respond to all the members of the group. For example, in a group of four, each member would get three charts.
2. Instruct students to take turns reading their couplets to the group.
3. After each student has read, have listeners think and then respond. Have them first respond in writing on the form, then orally to the reader.
4. Ask students to give the written response form to the reader after discussion is finished.

After students have used the charts to make revisions, you can collect the charts to evaluate students' growth in giving positive helpful feedback. Following is a completed sample Conferring and Responding to Writing Chart.

Conferring and Responding to Writing

	WRITING RESPONSE CHART
Response Topics:	**Name of Author:** _____ **Name of Responder:** _____
1. Encouragement—my favorite part was…	*I could see you standing next to the swings. I liked comparison to a cup full of water.*
2. I would like to know…	*why you didn't say anything to them.*
3. I liked the words…	*"water" and "daughter"—they rhyme.*
4. You might want to…	*find a rhyme for "full"—maybe "pull."*

Ask students if they think rhyming is worth the trouble. Does it help them say what they want to say better or does it get in the way? Do they have to say things just because they fit the rhyme scheme?

Extension: If you get good results, you might combine some of the couplets into a class poem. Have students illustrate each couplet and form the pages into a class book.

▼ **Ode to My Socks, by Pablo Neruda, translated by Robert Bly** _____

Before You Read   **Student Edition p. 24**

Activity Master 7

Exploring Your Own Experience: Favorite Clothes Interview and Tally

- **Interview:** Pair students to interview one another about their favorite articles of clothing, then place two pairs together. Ask students to share their partners' favorites with the group of four.

- **Tally:** Have representatives of the groups report to the whole class to make a class tally of the most favorite articles of clothing. You or a student can record the numbers on a chart large enough for the whole class to see.

- **Bar Graph:** Ask pairs or groups of students to convert the tally into a bar graph.

ACTIVITY MASTER #7

Use with student text page 24.

Favorite Clothes Interview

Directions:

1. Interview a partner about his or her favorite article of clothing. Ask your partner questions such as:
    What is your favorite article of clothing?
    Would you please describe it?
    How did you get it?
    When do you wear it?
    Why do you like it so much?

2. Share what your partner told you with a small group or the class.

3. Make a class tally and graph of which articles of clothing are the "favorite" of most classmates. Use the chart and graph sample below.

FAVORITE CLOTHES						
Article of Clothing:	Shirt	Pants	Shoes	Hat	_____	_____
Tally:	2	3	4	5		
Graph: (Fill in up to the total tallied)						

Extension 1: Ask students to write a brief narrative to accompany the bar graph. The narrative could include an explanation of the process the class used to gather the information as well as a summary of the graph results.

Extension 2:   Have students work in pairs to create another type of graph to represent the results of the clothes tally, such as a pie chart or a line graph. Students could also use illustrations or other original methods of representation.

Student Edition p. 25

Reading the Poem: The length of this poem and its vocabulary make it very challenging. You may wish to use the suggestions on "rendering" the poem "We Wear the Mask" as listed on p. 26 of this Teacher's Guide, or try chunking as follows.

Chunking: Read the poem in logical "chunks." Since the poem is a series of similes, remind the students of work they have already done on similes (Student Edition p. 16). Assign pairs of students a "chunk" and ask them to illustrate their simile. Have students memorize their "chunks." Ask the class then to recite the poem in sequence as each pair displays the illustration they have created.

 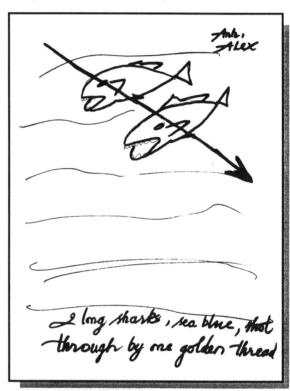

Student Illustrations of "Ode to My Socks"

Student Edition p. 26

Art Notes

"Illustration," by H. Bonner

Discussion suggestions:

1. Ask students to describe the painting. Do the socks look comfortable? What kinds of feelings do the students get when looking at the work? Are the colors warm or cold? Are they simple or complicated?
2. Ask students to match the images in the painting to images in the poem.
3. Relate the symmetry in this painting to symmetry in the Lois Mailou Jones painting.

After You Read

Student Edition p. 30

What Do You Think?   You may wish to follow some of the suggestions in *What Do You Think?* for "My moccasins have not walked," Teacher's Guide p. 18.

Activity Master 8

Try This: Cluster Map. It is important for students to become familiar with a variety of methods for brainstorming and organizing their ideas before writing. Point out to students that a cluster map can be used for brainstorming ideas in a variety of situations such as reports, science projects, or history papers. An article of clothing may not be an inspiring "turn-on" for some students. Since this cluster map is a brainstorm for an ode that students will write, it is important that students truly feel passionate about their topic, so allow students to choose. Other topics might be a favorite object (pen, car, basketball), a place in nature (river, mountain), or a person.

Student Edition p. 31

Learning About Literature: Rhythm in Poetry. Remind students of the rhythm they studied in "We Wear the Mask." You may wish to review the stressed and unstressed syllables of the poem. Demonstrate on the chalkboard or overhead the stressed and unstressed syllables in "My moccasins have not walked."

Extension: Ask students to compare the pattern of the three poems, "We Wear the Mask," "My moccasins have not walked," and "Ode to My Socks." Ask students in pairs to write a line using regular meter and irregular meter. Pairs can share their results with the class.

Writing: Have students read their rough drafts in small groups for feedback. To assist students in becoming skilled at giving positive feedback, see the suggestions for "We Wear the Mask," on p. 28 of this Teacher's Guide. The Response form for "Ode to My Socks" can include space to respond to the use of similes. You may wish to have students illustrate their poems and produce a class book of odes.

▼ The Raiders Jacket, by Gary Soto

Before You Read

Student Edition p. 32

Activity Master 9

Exploring Your Own Experience: Sunshine Outline. Discuss the questions on p. 32 of the Student Edition. Help students use **Activity Master #9** to outline their experience of having borrowed something. Make a transparency from the outline to help you model and describe its use.

Alternate Management Strategies

- **Language Experience.** Elicit student responses and write them on your Sunshine Outline transparency on the overhead projector as a full group activity.

- **Think–Pair–Share:** First, give students a few minutes of silence to think about and respond to questions individually. Then have each student share his or her response with a partner. Then have two pairs of students join up and ask each student to tell about his or her partner's response to the group of four. If you wish, ask volunteers to share their story with the whole class.

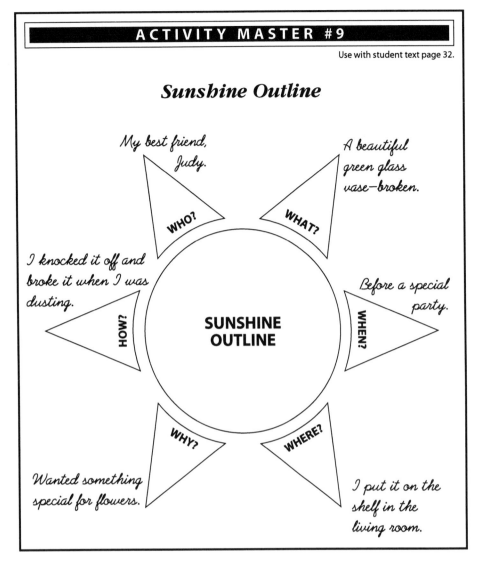

Sunshine Outline

My best friend, Judy.

WHO?

A beautiful green glass vase—broken.

WHAT?

I knocked it off and broke it when I was dusting.

HOW?

SUNSHINE OUTLINE

Before a special party.

WHEN?

Wanted something special for flowers.

WHY?

WHERE?

I put it on the shelf in the living room.

Student Edition p. 33

Reading the Story: Sections of this story contain a lot of dialogue. You may wish to assign roles to students for oral reading.

Student Edition p. 34

Art Notes

Photograph of girl in window

Discussion suggestions:

1. Ask students to describe the mood and setting of the photograph. Why is the woman looking out of the window? What do her facial expressions suggest she is thinking? Is the woman waiting for someone to come inside, or does she want to go outside? Is it an old house or new house? (The chipped paint suggests that the house is older.)
2. Ask students how the photograph illustrates the story.
3. Have students imagine the photograph with no windows. Would that change the mood of the picture?

Student Edition p. 40

Art Notes

"Bauhaus Stairway," by Oskar Schlemmer, 1932

Background:

Oskar Schlemmer (1888-1943), painter, sculptor, and stage designer, was a member of the famous German art school known as Bauhaus. The Bauhaus school of design, a powerful influence on contemporary art and architecture, taught that the arts should meet the needs of society and that fine arts and practical crafts were both art.

Discussion suggestions:	1. Do the figures look similar to or different from one another? What makes them look alike?
	2. Ask students if this painting looks like the mall that they like to go to.
	3. Tell students that Schlemmer was known for making paintings where the human figures look like dolls. Do they see dolls in the painting? Why or why not?
	4. Ask students what, if anything, makes the painting interesting even when no faces are shown.

Student Edition p. 42

Art Notes

"Dutch Cheeses, Bread and Knife," artist and date unknown

Background:

This painting is called a "still life." It is a painting of objects that are arranged by the artist. Unlike other "realistic" paintings that portray nature landscapes, still lifes are almost always set indoors and contain at least one man-made object.

Discussion suggestions:

1. Is this painting more or less exciting than *"Les Fetiches"*? Why?
2. Ask students if this picture makes them hungry.
3. How do the style and subject of the painting relate to the ending of the story?

After You Read

Student Edition p. 44

What Do You Think?   Have students work in small groups. You can jigsaw the questions, assigning groups different questions. Ask students to share their thoughts about the questions with the whole class.

You may wish to try a "Character Chair" if you need a new approach to the post-reading questions. This enables students to understand the motives, or reasons why, characters act as they do. Use the following five steps to complete a "character chair."

1. Place three chairs in the front or center of the room. Ask for volunteers to be the main characters in the story—Lorena, Eddie, and Guadalupe.
2. Ask the rest of the students to think of questions they would like to ask the characters from the story. Model for students by writing some of the questions on the board. The focus should be on **why**-questions.
3. Tell students to work on their own and write two or three questions for each character. If they need more **why**-question models, have them use the questions in the *What Do You Think?* section. These questions can be altered and expanded upon to help students develop the discussion. For example, the question, "Why do you think Eddie loaned Lorena the jacket?" (p. 44) can be reworded by the students as "Eddie, why did you loan Lorena the jacket?"
4. Have students address their questions to the characters in the chairs.
5. Remind students in the chairs to use the evidence from the story. Have them try to stay in character. Model by playing the role of a character for a short time. If a character becomes "stuck," allow other students to provide responses. The purpose of the activity is to promote lively discussion, not to put someone uncomfortably on the spot.

Student Edition p. 44

Try This: Cause and Effect.   Extend this jigsaw activity by having the groups share their information with the class. Two alternative ways for sharing follow.

   a) **Language Experience Activity:**   Ask representatives from each group to report to the whole class. You or a student can write cause and effect sentences on the chalkboard or a chart.

b) **Group-to-Group Activity:** Rotate the Cause and Effect charts through the groups. As each group gets a "day," they write a few sentences showing cause and effect. For example, "Because Eddie lets Lorena borrow the jacket for one day, everybody thinks he likes her." Rotate the charts until each group has had an opportunity to work with all the "days."

Student Edition p. 46

Activity Master 10

Learning About Literature: Character Development. Students' answers will vary from the following Character Development Chart.

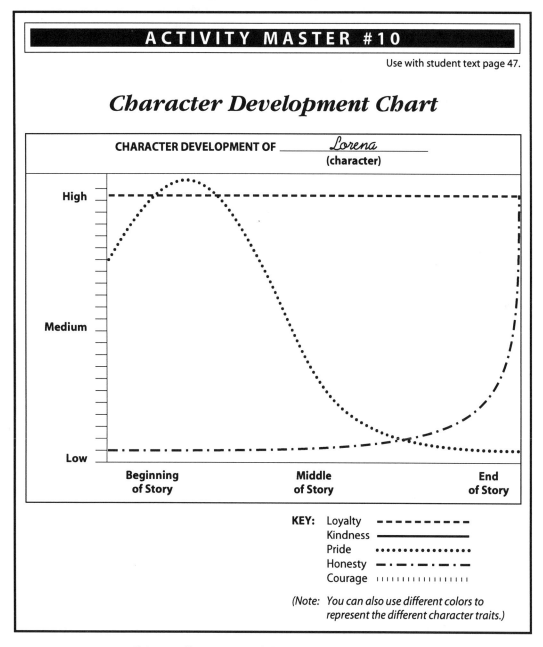

ACTIVITY MASTER #10

Use with student text page 47.

Character Development Chart

CHARACTER DEVELOPMENT OF _____*Lorena*_____
(character)

High

Medium

Low

Beginning of Story — Middle of Story — End of Story

KEY: Loyalty – – – – – – – –
Kindness ─────────
Pride •••••••••••••••
Honesty – • – • – • – • –
Courage ıııııııııııııııı

(Note: You can also use different colors to represent the different character traits.)

Walking Gallery: Extend this activity by grouping the character charts for the same characters together and posting them. Have students tour the charts. Make students accountable for their tour by taking notes on what they find interesting and which characters appeared to change the most.

Writing: Point out to students that their discussions, writing, and charts will help them formulate their ideas for their character sketch.

▼ The Dress Mess, by Del Stover

Before You Read

Student Edition p. 48

Activity Master 11

Exploring Your Own Experience: Dress Code Interviews. You may wish to have students interview members of their community. Spend time preparing students so they have a clear idea of whom they will interview and what questions will be asked before beginning the assignment. If you have students interview one another in the classroom, here are two suggestions:

a) If your students come from a variety of countries, ask them to choose interviewees from a culture different from their own.

b) If you have only a few ethnic groups represented, ask students of the same culture to work together to create a chart similar to the one on Student Edition p. 48. The information from the charts created by student groups can be combined into one class chart.

Use with student text page 48.

Dress Code Survey Data Chart

Name and location of school	Does the school have uniforms or other dress code?	What are the consequences of not following the code?	What is the effect of the dress code on your behavior and schoolwork?	What is the effect on other students' behavior and schoolwork?
Guatemala	None	—	—	—
San Pedro, Mexico	Uniforms: white and blue	Go home and change	Proud to be student	Not worry about who is rich
Maryhurst, Oregon	Uniforms: gray and white	Demerits	Behaved; school pride	School pride
School 5, Vietnam	Uniforms: blue and white	Stand with arms out	Worked hard	Some worked harder, some not
Vietnam	Uniforms	Call parents	—	—
Mexico	Code	Demerits	Good for studying	Pride
St. Michael, Guatemala	Uniforms: green and gold	Go home	Not worry about clothes	Work hard
Craft School, Nigeria	Uniforms	Cut grass	Proud of school	None
School 6, Russia	Uniforms	Lose points	Good	Good
Technical School, Ukraine	Uniforms	Parents called to come to school	Good	Good
Kennedy, New York	Code: no hats	Take off hat or see vice principal	None	None

Student Edition p. 50

Art Notes

Photograph: "Students at a school near Dar-es Salaam, Tanzania, Africa"

Discussion suggestions:

Have the students look at the picture carefully. Ask them to find the differences among the students: how does each student express her individuality even though she wears the same colors?

After You Read

Student Edition p. 52

Activity Master 12

Try This: Outlining the Article with a Chart. Student answers may vary from the following sample **Activity Master #12 (Uniforms and Dress Codes Chart).**

Uniforms and Dress Codes Chart

Group	Why are uniforms or dress codes a good idea?	Why are uniforms or dress codes not a good idea?
Elementary school students	Proud of way they look, come ready to learn.	
High school students	50% are interested	50% not interested—concerned about individuality.
Principals	Have fewer discipline problems; kids behave.	
Teachers	Reduce competition over clothes.	
Parents	Economic necessity, save money with basic look.	Uniforms cost more than basic look.
School board	Reduce competition, reduce crime over clothes, required all schools have uniform policy.	

Student Edition p. 53

Writing: Writing an Essay. To help students develop a method for organizing their writing, ask students to make a two-column chart, or *т-chart,* of evidence in support of and against dress codes or uniforms. You may wish to make a chart as a class as follows:

T-Chart: In Support of and Against Dress Codes in the School

Support	Against
Save money on clothes.	Look like everyone else.
Reduce competition in clothes.	Not comfortable all seasons.
Students look neat.	Won't look good in the style.
Students more willing to work.	Want to express self.
Eliminate gang dressing and perhaps gang behavior.	Problems changing schools—different uniform needed.
Build pride in school.	Hard to enforce—gives one more rule to break or rebel against.

Ask students to tell if they are in support of or against dress codes or uniforms and to write their essays based on their beliefs.

Student Feedback: See p. 28 for suggestions on student feedback groups. Alternatively, you may wish to do the following:

1. Assign each student a number so that students may remain anonymous.
2. Place students' anonymous, numbered writing in a central location and provide feedback forms (use **Activity Master #6,** or create your own form).
3. Instruct students to read several papers and give written feedback.
4. The feedback can be attached to the paper or given to the authors at the end of the period. Each paper should receive feedback from several students.

Extension 1: You may wish to have students brainstorm other topics about which they have strong feelings and write essays supporting their opinions. The essays can be sent to newspapers or school officials, or perhaps combined into a class publication.

Extension 2: Have students debate the issue of uniforms in their school.

Unit Follow-Up: Making Connections

Student Edition p. 54

Unit Project Hints

1. Go over all the projects so students understand what each involves. Encourage questions.
2. Ask each student to select a project by writing his or her name and the project number on a slip of paper. Encourage students to make different choices from those of their friends. Students can also create their own ideas for projects and have them approved by you.
3. Use the slips of paper to make group assignments. Limit groups to four people.
4. Clearly specify the dates that different stages of the project are due and your expectations for format.
5. With group projects, have students include individual, private reports on what role each student played and how effectively the group operated. Students may use **Activity Master #15 (Group Project Evaluation).**

Student Edition p. 55

Activity Master 16

Further Reading: Give a copy of **Activity Master #16 (Further Reading for Unit 1: Style)** to your school librarian and ask him or her to help you find and/or purchase the materials for the library so that they will be available to your students. Ask the librarian for other recommendations. Add your own and those of your students to a copy of the *Further Reading* list for Unit 1. Reproduce the list for students to use in selecting outside reading. Provide silent reading time in class for students to read the materials.

Encourage students to start a literary journal in which they record the titles and authors of the books they read along with the dates they finished and their thoughts about the book. Offer to read the journals and write responses to students. Consider offering extra credit or other motivations for students to keep up their literary journals.

Technology Note: Have students keep electronic journals. You can respond to them electronically using word processor files or by sending "journal-type" messages using messaging software or e-mail.

Assessment Opportunities for Students in Unit 1: Style

You may wish to refer to p. 11 of the Teacher's Guide to review the philosophy and management strategies for evaluation and assessment in *Voices.* Sample checklists for evaluation are in the Appendix of this guide. You may adapt and expand these lists for your students. It is important that students have a clear idea of what is expected of them and what standards of performance constitute progress. Share the assessment criteria with your students. In addition to recording students' progress on the checklists, you may wish to have students track their own growth in the areas of oral/aural language, reading, writing, and group participation. Students can record their own progress on checklists similar to those in the Appendix in this Teacher's Guide and keep them in their portfolios. Students can also create their own standards for good performance. Students know quality. Following is an example of a middle school student-created evaluation chart for written projects. In teacher-led activities, students brainstormed and categorized the assessment items, then used the chart to assess their performance throughout the year. The chart contains room for teacher, peer, and self-evaluation.

SELF & PEER EVALUATION

Writer _____

Evaluator _____

Date _____

	SELF		PEER		TEACHER	
	Strong	Needs to Improve	Strong	Needs to Improve	Strong	Needs to Improve
CONTENT						
1. Interesting, artistic or creative						
2. Exciting words/vocabulary						
3. Beginning, middle, end/organization						
4. Title						
5. Easy to understand/makes sense						
6. Details						
7. Adjectives						
MECHANICS						
1. Spelling						
2. Complete and correct sentences						
3. Capital letters						
4. Punctuation						
5. Correct paragraph or writing form						
OTHER						
1. Effort (is the writer trying?)						
2. Is the paper finished on time?						
3. Nice handwriting						
4. Overall neatness and presentation						
5. Good preparation before writing						
6. Cooperation during group projects						

Idea from Angela Gadbois

In the *Assessment Opportunities* section concluding each unit in the Teacher's Guide, we have included suggestions for assessing oral/aural language development, reading, writing, group participation, and content. The beginning of the term is the time to collect baseline information on students so you can assess them, and they can evaluate themselves, on their individual progress. Take advantage of the following opportunities to collect data in Unit 1.

1. **Oral/Aural Skills:** Collect a recording of students' reading or reciting. Following are some suggestions.

   a) Have each student be responsible for his or her own audio or video cassette tape. When you record the student, use two recorders or video cameras. Place your composite tape of the whole class in one machine and have the student place his or her tape in the other. The student can keep his or her personal tape in a portfolio, and compare the progress made during the year. Set the criteria for progress. You can use an analytic rating system considering such items as clarity of ideas, pronunciation, style, and pragmatic strategies. Here is an example:

Spoken Language Description

	Clarity of Ideas	Pronunciation/ Mechanics	Style/ Fluency	Pragmatics/ Strategy
1	Jumbled, disorganized.	Too soft or loud.	Remote, isolated from audience.	Gives up after one try.
2	Speech conveys simple meaning limited to concrete or survival topic.	May not be able to make sounds that don't occur in L1.	May show timidity, but overcomes it.	Keeps trying, but may only have one strategy (e.g., repeating, or loudness).
3	Topics are more abstract, of general interest.	Student can produce all English sounds, usually uses them appropriately.	Effort required to express meaning is less evident.	Begins to try a variety of strategies: gestures, circumlocution, etc.
4	Student can combine ideas to form a short line of argument or more complex thought.	Speech is understood by most people.	Student seems at ease, shows no fear.	Uses more strategies to accomplish task (e.g., rewording, gestures, emotional appeals).
5	Vocabulary is rich enough to express virtually all thoughts.	Speech is easily understood.	Flowing speech—meaning is not impeded by breaks.	Uses language effectively to meet needs and express desires, opinions.

   b) Observe groups during activities such as Think–Pair–Share or Round Table to check students' oral participation. Use the Oral/Aural Language Checklist in the Teacher's Guide Appendix, p. 98, to keep records. This information can be collected in class in one week by observing a few students for a few minutes each day. Ask students to tape their group discussion to assess their own growth in oral skills.

2. **Writing:** Have students organize writing folders for works in progress. Then have them staple the **Editing Checklist (Activity Master #14)** and the **Conferring and Responding to Writing** chart **(Activity Master #6)** to the back of the folder, and highlight concepts as you cover them in class. (You may adapt and expand these charts for your students.) Have students staple a **Status of Writing Chart**

(see Appendix, p. 102) to the front of the folder. This will help both you and the student keep track of works in progress. Works from all steps of the writing process should be saved in the writing folder, including products of prewriting activities such as clustering, mapping, or illustrating. You and the students can use these baseline inclusions for comparison with later works to assess growth in both written language and use of the writing process.

3. **Reading:** To demonstrate that they understand the use of simile, have students find examples of similes in a favorite song or poem and explain what is being compared.

4. **Group Work:** Save samples of students' **Group Project Evaluation** charts (**Activity Master #15**) to keep track of both how students observe their own group process and how others observe them participating. These charts can be compared with later participation charts.

5. **End-of-Unit Projects:** The *Unit Follow-Up: Making Connections* section at the end of every unit offers opportunity for assessment in all areas. Develop and present to students criteria for the evaluation of their projects. If more than one student has chosen the same project, you can have students brainstorm and set criteria for what they think is an excellent, average, or poor result. Or you may work with the whole class to set criteria for written, oral, and art projects. These could be used for the rest of the year.

UNIT 2: SUSPENSE

	Student Edition pp. 56–57
Art Notes	Unit Opener: *"La Bonne Adventure,"* by René Magritte
Background:	René Magritte (1898–1967), born in Belgium, lived in Brussels all his life, except for a short stay in Paris. His painting is "surrealist," which is "magic realism." Surrealists borrow their images from dreams and visions. Magritte wrote that "dreams...are not intended to make you sleep but wake you up."
Discussion suggestions:	1. Ask students to describe the mood of the painting. What about it might make them think of "suspense"?
	2. Ask students if this house looks like their houses. Why or why not?
	3. Ask students to guess why the moon might be in the lower left-hand corner. Is this a picture of the houses on land? In the sky? Or both? Ask them to guess what Magritte might have meant by placing stars and the moon not above the houses but in them. Is the painting set in the evening, as the gray sky would suggest? Or at night? Can a painting show two times at once? Two places at once?

▼ The Ghost's Bride, from *The Rainbow People,* by Laurence Yep ————————

Before You Read	**Student Edition p. 58**
	Activity Master 17
	Exploring Your Own Experience: Wedding and Marriage Customs. Activity **Master #17** contains guidelines for students' interviews of parents or grandparents about their weddings. Students may not live with parents or grandparents, so be sure to suggest alternative persons to interview, for example, persons from their culture working in the school, relatives, or older members of their cultural community. Have students plan whom they will interview and rehearse questions they will ask. Students may choose or need to conduct the interviews in languages other than English. You may wish to fill out a chart to share with students. Students' answers will vary from the following sample.

Wedding and Marriage Customs

Interview Questions	Answers
Who decides who will marry?	The bride and groom choose whom they will marry.
How do people get ready for the wedding?	The man usually buys a diamond engagement ring, which he gives the woman before the wedding. The bride and groom and the families plan where to have the ceremony and whom to invite.
Who pays for what?	The bride's family pays for the wedding, and the groom's family pays for a dinner before the wedding. The other members of the wedding ceremony pay for clothes they wear in the ceremony.
What are the wedding ceremonies like?	Sometimes they are in a church, sometimes a park or hall by a justice of peace. Ceremonies vary depending on the religion of the couple.
What kinds of parties are held?	There is a dinner for both families before the wedding, and reception for everyone attending the wedding after. Sometimes the bride's friends give her a special party and presents at a "shower" before the wedding.
Where do the bride and groom live afterwards?	They live where they choose.
How old are the bride and groom, usually?	They are usually in their 20s.

Extension: Have students choose cultures other than their own. Ask them to write reports about the marriage customs of chosen cultures based on the information from the charts.

Student Edition pp. 59–64

Reading the Story: Creating suspense is the focus of *Learning About Literature* for this selection (p. 67). To prepare students for this discussion, you can do one of the following:

- **Read Aloud:** Stop at various points in the story. Ask students what they are wondering about and what they think will happen. Record the questions and comments on chalkboard, chart, or overhead.

- **Silent Reading:** Ask students to record their questions and predictions on self-stick notes or in journals as they read the story.

- **Paired Reading:** Ask pairs of students to record their questions and predictions as they alternate reading the story. Have the partner not reading a question and make a prediction.

Student Edition p. 60

Art Notes

"Landscape in the Style of Huang Kung-wang," by Wang Yuan-chi, 1706

Background:

Wang Yuan-chi was the youngest of the famous "Four Wangs" who dominated painting during the Ch'ing dynasty. Wang Yuan-chi was a scholar as well as a painter; here he works in the style of another painter, Huang Kung-wang (1269–1354).

Discussion suggestions:

1. Ask students to describe the feeling this painting gives them. Peaceful? Adventurous?
2. Does this landscape remind students of a place they've been to?
3. Have students find another painting in the book (Rufino Tamayo's "Boy in Blue," p. 206, is one choice) with almost the exact same palette. A palette is both the actual board upon which painters mix paints and a term for the range and variety of colors in a work. Why might an eighteenth-century painter have such a simple palette (dyes were still naturally based)? Why might Tamayo, a twentieth-century painter, choose the same palette?

Student Edition p. 62

Art Notes

"Night View of Matsuchiyama and the San'ya Canal," by Utagawa Hiroshige

Background:

Utagawa Hiroshige (1797–1858) was born in Edo (now Tokyo) to a family of humble station in the eighth year of the Kansei reform period in Japan. Both he and his father were firemen. The prints of another artist, Hokusai, inspired Hiroshige to study art. Studying under Utagawa Toyohiro (from whom he took his professional name, Utagawa), he was the last great figure of Ukiyo-e ("pictures of the floating world"), the popular Japanese school of art and printmaking in Japan during the Edo period.

Discussion suggestions:

1. Before they read the story, ask students if the woman looks scary or ghostly to them. After reading the story, do they change their minds?
2. Ask students to compare this woman to other pictures of women in the book. How are they alike? Different?
3. How do students compare the Chinese painting on p. 60 to the Japanese painting on p. 62? What subject and style differences do they notice? Do both relate to the story?

After You Read

Student Edition p. 66

What Do You Think? Use a jigsaw activity for question 2 of *What Do You Think?* on p. 66. Assign pairs or groups of students different characters to study. Then ask representatives from each group to share the group's results with the class.

Activity Master 18

Try This: Culture Map. You may wish to have students gather information on Kwangtung (Guangdong) Province. Students can infer information for the chart based on their knowledge of Kwangtung as well as from the story. Students' answers will vary from the following sample culture map.

Use with student text page 66.

Culture Map

Questions	Answers
Name of culture?	Chinese.
Where do the people live?	Rural China, in small villages that are not too far from each other—within walking distance.
What is the land like?	
What is the climate like?	
Who lives together?	It is a close community where people help each other. For a wedding, consent of the parents is asked. Then the bride, who brings food, is picked up in a sedan chair. She is brought to the house of the groom. He is offered water to wash with. Then there is a marriage feast.
How do people make a living?	People are farmers and have small shops in the villages. Success means having food and basic necessities of life.
How does the group practice religion?	When people die, their spirits live on as ghosts. Life after death is similar to life on earth. Ghosts remain near the places where they lived and can be communicated with.
How do people stay healthy?	People's health can be affected by spirits. Special wise persons know how to heal. They rely on their knowledge of herbs as well as their understanding of human nature and the history of the people of the area.
Who are the leaders? How do people make decisions?	Wise persons help the villagers and farmers decide what to do. People are well organized and help each other through difficulties.

Extension: Reader's Theater. If possible, take your students to a play or watch a video performed by other students. Talk to your students about what makes a good performance. They will bring up ideas such as loud and clear speech, good eye contact, interesting characterization, actions consistent with the character, good props and costumes, all actors knowing when it is their turn to speak, and so on. List these ideas on a chart to display in the classroom. Refer to the chart when helping students prepare their skits.

This story has six characters (narrator, mother, daughter, wise woman, ghost, dead girl's mother) and an option for as many minor characters as you need for each student to participate (e.g., sedan carriers, wedding guests). If possible, videotape the performance for later discussion of what went well and what might be improved.

Before You Read

Student Edition p. 68

Exploring Your Own Experience: Think–Pair–Share.   To help create a spooky mood while students are thinking, you can play scary or spooky sounds. The audio cassette "The Haunted House" or other scary Halloween sounds may be available through your school media center or public library. Ask groups to share with the class some of the spooky sounds they know. Make a class chart of these words or phrases as a resource for students to use later during the writing activity.

Student Edition p. 69

Background: While reading the poem, you may wish to use suggestions for "rendering" on p. 26. Have students copy the poem on one page so that they have a visual image of the use of space in the poem. They can mark those word patterns that they find interesting on the copy. Alternately, have students use self-stick notes in the text to mark interesting words or phrases.

Student Edition p. 70

Art Notes

"The Scream," by Edvard Munch, 1893

Background:

Edvard Munch (1863–1944) was born in central Norway. He rejected the emotionally neutral subjects of impressionism (see, for example, the Matisse paintings on pp. 12, 100, and 184). His brooding, anguished expressionistic painting and graphic works were based on his personal grief and obsession over the deaths of his mother and sister from tuberculosis when he was a child. In 1892 his exhibition so shocked the authorities that they closed it down.

Discussion suggestions:

1. How does this painting convey "suspense"? What does the central figure look like? A skeleton? The boy Macaulay Culkin played in *Home Alone*? (The boy's facial expression was modeled after this painting.) Who are the two figures in the upper-left?
2. Ask students why the figure is screaming. Have students relate the painting to the poem.
3. Point out to students how the sky and water are painted as if they were moving and how the walkway is painted at such an angle that the figure appears to be ready to fall out of the painting. How do these elements contribute to a sense of suspense?

After You Read

Student Edition p. 72

What Do You Think?   Question 3 asks students why e.e. cummings signs his name the way he does. After students have an opportunity to offer their thoughts, share the following information with them. The use of lower-case letters in cummings' name came about because a printer mistakenly typeset it that way in a 1917 publication, *Eight Harvard Poets*. e.e. cummings continued to use that form. Of course, the rest of the unconventional punctuation and spelling were intentional on the part of the poet.

Student Edition p. 72

Activity Master 19

Try This: Word Pairs and Patterns.   Your students may find more examples of word pairs and patterns than on the following sample chart.

Word Pairs and Patterns

First Word	Second Word	Changes
hoppy	happy	"o" changed to "a"
toad	tweed	middle letters changed
itchy	twitchy	"tw" dropped
nose	knows	same sound, different spelling
ooch	ach	"oo" changed to "a"
great	green	"ea" changed to "ee"

Student Edition p. 73

Activity Master 20

Learning About Literature: If your students are interested in examining more of the tools cummings used besides free verse, direct them to Student Edition Appendix B, *Guide to Literary Terms and Techniques,* pp. 242–247, to find definitions for repetition, alliteration, assonance, and parallelism. You may wish to jigsaw this activity by assigning pairs of students to find examples of each sound device. Follow up by making a class chart of all the sound devices and post the chart as a place for students to add sound devices throughout the year.

Sound Devices in Poetry

NAME OF DEVICE	DEFINITION	EXAMPLES
Repetition	Repeated use of a sound, word, phrase, sentence, rhythm, or grammatical pattern	Examples in "hist whist": *bob-a-nob bob-a-nob* *the devil ooch/the devil/ach the great* *green/dancing/devil/devil/devil/devil*
Alliteration	Repetition of initial consonant sounds Examples in "Ode to My Socks": *Maru Mori* *socks as soft* *save them somewhere as schoolboys* *for pieces of pink*	Examples in "hist whist": *hoppy happy* *tip-toe/twinkle-toe* *toad in tweeds/tweeds* *whisk look out for the old woman/with the wart* *great/green* *dancing/devil* Example in "We Wear the mask": *mouth with myriad*
Assonance	Repetition of vowel sounds	Examples in "hist whist": *with scuttling eyes/rustle and run* *little twitchy witches and tingling/goblins* *little itchy mousies* Example in "My moccasins have not walked": *fondled the spotted fawn*
Parallelism	Repetition of grammatical patterns Examples in "Ode to My Socks": *two socks as soft/two long sharks* *two immense blackbirds/two cannons* *I resisted/I resisted*	Example in "hist whist": *tip toe/twinkle toe* Examples in "My moccasins have not walked": *My moccasins have not/My medicine pouch has not/My hands have not/My eyes have not/My hair has not* Example in "We Wear the Mask": *We wear the mask (repeated after each stanza)*

Student Edition p. 73

Writing: Remind students that as they are becoming more proficient writers, they are learning strategies for helping them generate ideas. Suggest to students that they try clustering, drawing pictures, doing quickwrites, or talking about their ideas with partners to help them generate ideas for their poems.

Have students use **Activity Master #29 (Responding to Poetry)** to discuss poetry in small groups.

Technology Note: Students can print their poems in several versions with different font styles and sizes. Have each student choose one version and explain how it is appropriate for the piece.

▼ The Wise Woman of Córdoba, retold by Francisco Hinojosa

Before You Read

Student Edition p. 74

Exploring Your Own Experience: Sharing Your Culture. Direct the students to "Folktales" in the *Guide to Literary Terms and Techniques*, Student Edition pp. 242–247, and to the explanation of folktales in *Learning about Literature*, p. 81 of the Student Edition. Discuss the elements of folktales. Ask students to consider those elements when discussing their folktale with their group.

Student Edition pp. 75–79

Reading the Story: You may wish to follow the suggestions for *Reading the Story* for "The Ghost Bride" listed on p. 44 of this Teacher's Guide.

Student Edition p. 76

Art Notes

"Portrait of Galicia Galant," by Frida Kahlo, 1927

Background:

Frida Kahlo (1907–1954) was the daughter of a Mexican of Spanish and Indian descent and a German Jew. Kahlo was preparing to enter medical school when she was in a car accident. She taught herself to paint during her recuperation. Much of her work mixes fantasy, autobiography, and self-portraiture.

Discussion suggestions:

1. Frida Kahlo's painting is a portrait of a person she knew. She tried to make it look realistic. Is Schlemmer's painting on page 40 the same kind? Do you think he is trying to be "realistic" or do all the individuals look the same somehow? Why aren't these paintings portraits? Since a portrait conveys a person's unique individuality or style, ask students to find descriptions of Kahlo's figure's unique style.
2. Does the figure look like a "Wise Woman"? Why? Why not?
3. Ask students to describe the mood of the painting. Which elements (color, form, the figure's expression) contribute to the mood?

Student Edition p. 78

Art Notes

"Sunset off coast of Ruegen (Germany) after a stormy day," by J.C.C. Dahl, 1818

1. This is one of the few European paintings in this book of a naturalistic, or realistic, style. Ask students if they like this piece. Why or why not?
2. Some critiques of realism suggest that it does not engage the imagination. Ask students how they use their imaginations when they look at this painting. Where is the boat going? Who is on board?
3. Does the ship look like the one in the story?

After You Read

Student Edition p. 80

Activity Master 21

Try This: Character Web. Your students' webs will vary from the following sample character web.

Character Web

Generous:
- Found husbands for girls.
- Gave dresses to poor ladies.
- Helped miners find silver.

Rich:
They found ten barrels of gold in her house.

Wise Woman

Magic:
Appeared different places, could fly, drew a magic ship.

Creative:
Figured out how to get out of jail in clever and creative way—drew a ship and sailed out.

Extension: A Mock Trial. Hold a mock trial of "The Wise Woman of Córdoba." Have students portray the Wise Woman, the Judge, prosecutors (lawyers who try to prove that she is guilty), defense (lawyers who try to prove that she in innocent), witnesses for the prosecutors and defense, and a jury. Prosecutors, defense, and witnesses should take all their evidence directly from the story. Establish ground rules for how much students can elaborate.

Student Edition p. 81

Learning About Literature: Foreshadowing. Ask students to find examples of foreshadowing in "Eleven" and "The Raiders Jacket" in Unit 1.

Writing: The stories your students write present an opportunity for a class folktale book. Students can revise, edit, and illustrate their stories. Your school library may be interested in adding a copy of your students' publication to its collection of short stories. Students can also share their folktales with social studies classes dealing with multicultural issues. Have students prepare a **Culture Map (Activity Master #18)** for their tales to include in the sharing. English classes studying folktales may also be interested in your students' stories.

▼ The Hitchhiker: Two versions, by Haruo Aoki and Douglas J. McMillan

Before You Read

Student Edition p. 82

Activity Master 22

Exploring Your Own Experience: Two-Column Chart

Extension: Tell a story from your own experience. For example: My mother's friend told me that this happened one night many years ago. She was alone in the house because her husband was working nights. She had gone to sleep about ten, but suddenly awoke when she felt an icy cold hand on her shoulder. She sat up, looked around, and noticed that it was one in the morning. She put her head back on the pillow. Again she felt the icy cold hand shaking her. She looked up, and in the doorway of the room she saw her son. He said, "I just wanted to say goodbye," and he disappeared. A few hours later she received a phone call that her son had been killed in a car crash about one in the morning.

You may wish to call on volunteers to tell their stories to the class or have students share stories in small groups.

Note: It is important to set a tone for open-minded discussion as ghosts play an important role in many cultures' belief systems. To promote intercultural communication, you can have students share their cultural beliefs about ghosts or spirits.

Model by writing a T-list on the chalk board or on a transparency for the overhead projector. Here is a sample of a T-list using **Activity Master #22:**

ACTIVITY MASTER #22

Use with student text pages 82, 130, 134, 142.

Two-Column Chart (T-List)

Things that make me want to believe the story:	*Things that make me doubt the story:*
My mother said it happened to her friend.	*I've never seen a ghost.*
The time of the death and when she saw the ghost were the same.	*No one else was home to see it.*
	She might have had a very realistic dream.
She was very close to her son.	

Student Edition p. 85

Art Notes

Photograph: "Mile Post 277, Blue Ridge Parkway, North Carolina"

1. Ask students to guess if this is a painting or a photograph. Why did they make their choice? (The red grass might suggest a painting; the trees in the upper right corner have the detail of a photograph.)
2. How does the photograph fit the setting of the story? What is around the bend in the upper right corner?
3. Does anything in the photograph make it look eerie?

After You Read

Student Edition p. 86

Activity Master 23

Try This: Comparing and Contrasting Stories Using a Venn Diagram: This activity can be done individually, in pairs, in small groups, or as a whole class with the teacher using an overhead to write on a transparency of the Venn Diagram. Before asking students to make a Venn Diagram comparing and contrasting the two stories, model how to use the diagram on the overhead projector or chalk board. Use an example that is common knowledge to the students, such as comparing and contrasting cats and dogs: cats meow, climb trees, purr; dogs bark, fetch, wag their tails; both have whiskers, walk on four legs, are kept as pets.

Your students' answers for the comparison will vary from the following sample Venn Diagram.

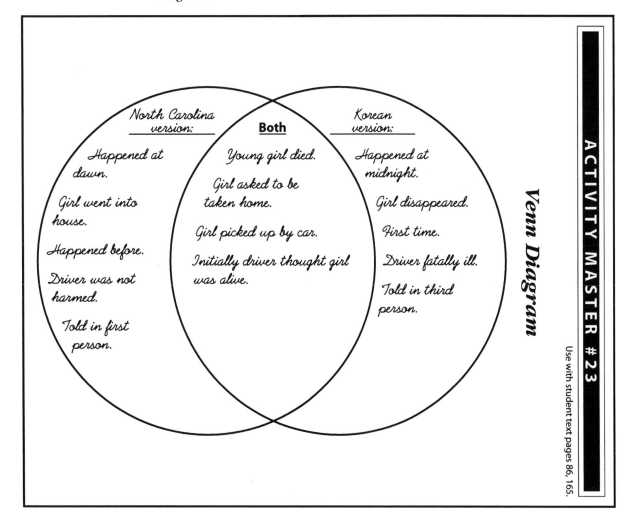

North Carolina version:
- Happened at dawn.
- Girl went into house.
- Happened before.
- Driver was not harmed.
- Told in first person.

Both
- Young girl died.
- Girl asked to be taken home.
- Girl picked up by car.
- Initially driver thought girl was alive.

Korean version:
- Happened at midnight.
- Girl disappeared.
- First time.
- Driver fatally ill.
- Told in third person.

Venn Diagram

ACTIVITY MASTER #23

Use with student text pages 86, 165.

Learning About Literature: Anecdotes

Extension: Story Board

1. Have student groups choose an interesting story to share with the whole class.
2. Have students make a story board. Ask them to divide a large piece of paper into four or six squares or "frames," depending on how many illustrations they want to make. In each square, have students illustrate a key event in the story.
3. Ask a representative of the group to tell the story using the story board as a reference. Alternately, have each member of the group tell a portion of the story using the story board as reference.
4. Remind students to explain what point, idea, or personality trait was revealed by the story.

Student Edition p. 87

Writing: Anecdotes.   Remind students that they have several strategies at their disposal to help organize their stories. They may wish to use a Sunshine Outline, a Story Board, or a Story Map to organize their thinking.

▼ The Wife's Story, by Ursula K. Le Guin

Before You Read   **Student Edition p. 88**

Background: "The Wife's Story" is a strange tale with an unusual twist in that the werewolf becomes a man. It has been chosen for *Voices* in part because the author, Le Guin, is popular among mainstream students. In building cultural understanding, we would like our ESL students to become aware of those authors popular with their peers.

If students are unfamiliar with werewolves, provide additional explanation. You might show a portion of a movie dealing with werewolves or read a short story to the class. (See *Further Reading*, Student Edition p. 109, for other suggestions.) Your school librarian may be able to assist you in finding an illustrated book about werewolves.

Reading the Story: The story is written in dialect. If you feel this will be problematic for your students, you might want to refer to *Before You Read* in Unit 4, "Mother to Son," Student Edition p. 190.

Students are asked in the section, *Try This: Draw the Setting,* p. 96, to draw a picture of the home as they imagined it before they knew who the wife and husband were. You may wish to read to p. 93 (before the werewolf turns into a man) and instruct students to turn books face down and draw what they think the home looks like. They can also predict the end of the story. What was the husband really doing?

Good readers construct meaning and make predictions as they read. Assist your students in becoming reflective readers by asking them to stop at key points in the story to offer opinions, describe what they see, predict what they think will happen, and check previous predictions.

Student Edition p. 90

Art Notes   Photograph of moon in forest

Discussion suggestions:

1. Ask students to describe the mood or feeling of this photograph. Do the trees seem real or unreal? Are the colors realistic or unrealistic? What do the colors resemble (a tie-dyed shirt, a rainbow)?
2. At what time of day do students think the photograph was taken? In what season? How can they tell?

3. How does the photograph relate to the story?

4. Compare this photograph with the previous photograph on p. 85. Which seems more realistic? Which is eerier? What is the relationship between things that seem unrealistic and suspenseful?

Student Edition p. 94

Art Notes

"Changeable Wolf/Man," by Ha So Da (Narciso Abeyta)

Background:

Ha So Da (Narciso Abeyta) is a Navajo, born in 1918 in Canoncito, New Mexico. He studied at the Santa Fe Indian School and the University of New Mexico. Ha So Da frequently chose subjects from Navajo mythology for his paintings, as is the case for "Changeable Wolf/Man." Of his own work, he comments: "I stuck with my own style of painting. I think what I concentrate on most is color."

Discussion suggestions:

1. Where is the "changeable wolf/man" in this picture? Why is the horse bucking?

2. Have students talk about the palette in this painting. Are the colors bold and exciting? How do the colors match the subject?

3. Point out how this painting lacks perspective (or depth). This at once makes the painting flat, but also gives the work a sense of motion, as the eye starts in the lower-left corner and moves up the canvas to the tree.

4. Ask students to find quotations in the story that relate to the art.

After You Read

Student Edition p. 96

Try This: Draw the Setting. If students have already drawn the home as they thought it was at the beginning of the story, have them now draw the home as they see it at the end of the story. After the groups have discussed their drawings, you can post the drawings and have a representative of each group give a summary of the group's discussion.

▼ The Raven, by Edgar Allen Poe

Before You Read

Student Edition p. 98

Exploring Your Own Experience: Round Table. In *Round Table,* have students work in groups of four, pass a paper around, and each take a turn adding a word to the list.

Hint: Have each student use a different color pen to enable you to quickly assess that each student has had an opportunity to contribute. You should see writing in four colors on the paper.

You can suggest that students think of what "sad" looks like or sounds like to help them generate words for the list.

Technology Note: Have students sit around a computer and create a list by taking turns typing a word.

Reading the Poem: "The Raven" is a very challenging poem. We have included it at the request of teachers who want ESL students exposed to some selections that frequently are included in the regular high school curriculum. If you decide to use it, you have the following choices in teaching it appropriately to your students:

• Have students read only the first stanzas, which are included in the unit itself.

• Have students read the entire poem, both the stanzas in the unit and the additional stanzas in Literary Appendix A (Student Edition pp. 230–232).

- Read the poem aloud several times to students, who can listen and enjoy the sounds. Don't expect them to understand the meaning of every word. You may have them mark those words or phrases whose sound is pleasing to them. (See "rendering," p. 26 of the Teacher's Guide.)
- Use a jigsaw activity. Form pairs of students and have each work on one stanza, find the meaning of each word, and paraphrase so that they understand. They can also illustrate the stanza to assist them in understanding it better as well as in sharing it. Work with each pair to keep them on track. Then have students share the meaning of each stanza with the class. Reread the whole poem aloud.
- Encourage students to accept this reading challenge independently.

Student Edition p. 100

Art Notes

"Still Life with Books," by Henri Matisse, 1890

Discussion suggestions:

1. Ask students what time of day the painting represents. How do they know?
2. Ask students to guess why an artist might want to create a painting that only shows books and newspapers. In making them an object of art, is he saying something about their importance?
3. Ask students why this painting was chosen to illustrate this poem. Which lines in the poem describe the art?

Student Edition p. 102

Art Notes

"Northern Raven," by John James Audubon

Background:

John James Audubon (1785–1851), born in Les Cays, Santo Domingo (now Haiti), studied drawing in France before he settled in Pennsylvania. In 1827, his masterpiece, *The Birds of America,* 435 hand-colored large folio pages with paintings of 1,065 life-sized birds, was published. Although he was a lover of birds, Audubon often killed the birds in order to study them for his paintings. The Audubon Society, an organization for the study and preservation of nature, is named for the painter.

Discussion suggestions:

1. Ask students to describe the illustration. Does the bird look scary? Or friendly?
2. Ask students to imagine that they had not read Poe's poem, but had come across this illustration in a field guide of birds. Would the bird still look scary? Why or why not?

After You Read

Student Edition p. 106

What Do You Think? You may find the discussion of *What Do You Think?* richer if you have students do the jigsaw activity of *Try This* first. You can ask students to illustrate their paraphrased stanzas.

Student Edition p. 107

Learning About Literature: Assonance. If your students are challenged by finding examples of assonance, have them find examples of alliteration first. Here are some examples:

...nodded, nearly napping	(Student Edition p. 99)
Doubting, dreaming dreams no mortal ever dared to dream	(Student Edition p. 103)

Provide each group with an audio cassette recording of the stanzas to help them hear examples of assonance. Some examples of assonance that your students may find are:

> ...midnight dreary,
> while I pondered, weak and weary (Student Edition p. 99)
>
> ...separate dying ember (Student Edition p. 99)
>
> ...sorrow
> for the lost Lenore (Student Edition p. 101)
>
> ...murmured back
> the word (Student Edition p. 103)

Student Edition p. 107

Learning About Literature: Rhyme Scheme. Jigsaw the stanzas of the poem: ask each group to write the rhyme scheme of one stanza. Make certain the groups understand where each stanza ends, and where the end of each line occurs. Ask groups to report their findings to the class and make a class chart of the rhyme scheme. Following is the rhyme scheme as illustrated by the second through fifth stanzas in the unit.

Stanza 2		Stanza 3		Stanza 4		Stanza 5	
December	a	*curtain*	a	*longer*	a	*fearing*	a
floor	b	*before*	b	*implore*	b	*before*	b
borrow	c	*repeating*	c	*rapping*	c	*token*	c
Lenore	b	*door*	b	*door*	b	*Lenore*	b
Lenore	b	*door*	b	*door*	b	*Lenore*	b
evermore	b	*more*	b	*more*	b	*more*	b

Extension: Explore with students the use of rhyme in the poetry of their native language. Have students work with others from the same country. You or the students may have access to books in students' native languages, or students may be able to write poems from memory. Ask a representative of each group to share with the class a summary of the group's discussion about rhyme scheme.

Unit Follow-Up: Making Connections

Student Edition p. 109

Activity Master 24

Further Reading: Use **Activity Master #24** to help students find outside reading related to the unit. Before copying and distributing the Activity Master, add your own suggestions for further reading, and ask your students and your librarian for recommendations to add to the list.

Assessment Opportunities for Students in Unit 2: Suspense

1. **Oral/Aural:** Video tape a performance of student Reader's Theater performance, for example, "The Ghost's Bride." Show it to the students and ask them to assess what they did well and what they would like to improve based on the criteria they set for good performance.

2. **Writing:** Ask each student to choose one piece of writing from his or her folder and take it through the writing process to publication. Assess students on effective use of stages of the process.

3. Reading:

a) Ask students to keep a reading log on one story they have read outside class. Have them record questions and make predictions similar to the way they did in "The Ghost Bride." Chart their progress on the Reading Checklist.

b) Ask students to find a favorite folktale and analyze it for the elements of a folktale.

4. Group Work:
Observe students working together in a Round Table activity or in the production of the Reader's Theater for "The Ghost's Bride." Record their progress on the Group Project Evaluation Chart and have students assess themselves using the Student Self-Assessment Form.

5. Content:
Ask students to demonstrate their understanding of comparison and contrast by using a Venn Diagram for an activity in another class. In history, for example, they could compare two political leaders; in science, they could compare two organisms, processes, or elements.

6. End-of-Unit Projects:
Use the projects at the end of the unit to assess student growth in speaking, listening, reading, and writing skills. Create criteria for evaluating the projects.

UNIT 3: LOVE

Student Edition pp. 110–111

Art Notes

Unit Opener: *"Chez le Père Lathuille,"* by Édouard Manet, 1879

Background:

Édouard Manet (1832-1883), born in Paris, was a French impressionist who refused that label. He went to sea with the merchant marines as a boy. Manet painted everyday subject matter with broad simple colors and vivid brush techniques. Manet was very interested in the impact of daylight on objects.

Discussion suggestions:

1. Ask students to describe the painting. How do they know the figures are in love? Do they find the colors interesting? Who do they "know" better, the man or the woman?
2. Ask students to compare this painting to the photograph of Maria and Tony on p. 152. How are they alike? Different?
3. Ask students to compare this painting to the cover painting by Tamayo. Point out how in this painting, we are looking at a man who is looking at a woman; in the Tamayo painting, we are looking at both a man and a woman. Do the paintings say similar or different things about men and women? About love?

▼ Although I Conquer All the Earth, Anonymous, from ancient India _____

Before You Read

Student Edition p. 112

Activity Master 25

Exploring Your Own Experience: Concentric Circles

Students' answers will vary from the following sample.

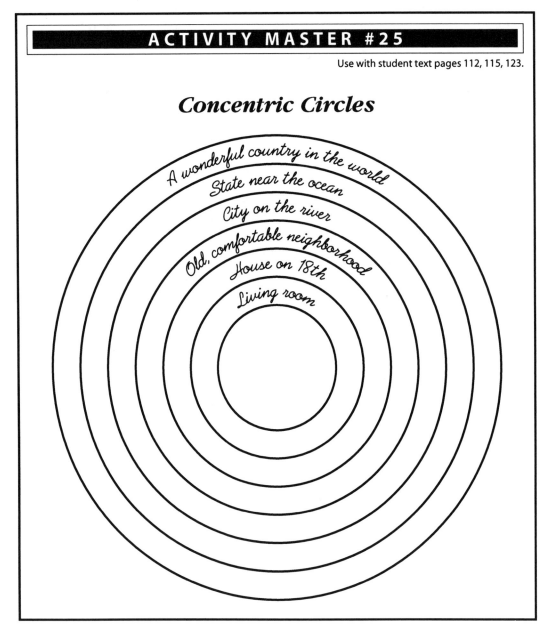

ACTIVITY MASTER #25

Use with student text pages 112, 115, 123.

Concentric Circles

A wonderful country in the world

State near the ocean

City on the river

Old, comfortable neighborhood

House on 18th

Living room

Student Edition p. 113

Art Notes   *"Desvarati Ragini,"* page from a dispersed Ragamala manuscript, 1605–6, India

Discussion suggestions:

1. Ask students if this art reminds them of other paintings in the book. Which ones? (Macke's use of color? Hiroshige's use of black outline for figures and intricate detail?) Why?
2. Ask students to relate the painting to the poem.
3. Have students guess what the woman is doing.

After You Read   **Student Edition p. 114**

What Do You Think?   You may wish to use the suggestions for alternative ways to answer the questions for *What Do You Think?* See Teacher's Guide p. 18.

Extension: We construct meaning from poetry through the words of the poet and through the life experiences we bring to the poem. To lead students to an understanding of this, try the following. Have each student illustrate one line (concentric circle) of the poem. There will be more than one illustration for each line of the poem, and the illustrations will be different from one another. For example, all students drawing it will not see the house. Discuss the differences and similarities in the drawings. Each student brings to the poem his or her experience of what a place looks like.

Student Edition p. 115

Activity Master 25

Try This: Using Parallel Structures. Use **Activity Master #25 (Concentric Circles).**

Writing: Review the writing process with students. Remind them that writing is not a single act; it is a multistep process that all authors go through. Have students keep **Activity Master #13 (The Writing Process)** in their writing folders for reference.

▼ Karate, from *The Land I Lost,* by Huynh Quang Nhuong

Before You Read

Exploring Your Own Experience: Think–Pair–Share. Think-Pair-Share is a three-step process. First, have students think about what they are going to say. Second, ask them to share their ideas with a partner. Third, have each pair get together with another pair and ask each student to tell the group what his or her partner said.

You may wish to help students organize their thinking for the first step of *Think-Pair-Share* by listing the topics for discussion on the chalkboard, a large piece of paper, or the overhead projector. It might look like this:

Roles of men	Roles of women	Roles of both	Roles of couples not typical

Have students refer to the list as they think about and share their ideas. After students have completed Step Three of the process, have them create a class chart. Ask representatives from each group to go to the chart and fill in one or more ideas. To save time, have students write their ideas on large self-stick notes to post on the chart.

Note: This is a good opportunity to promote intercultural communication by discussing different cultures' expectations of roles in marriage.

Student Edition p. 118

Art Notes

"Night View of Saruwaka-machi," by Utagawa Hiroshige (1797–1858)

Discussion suggestions:

1. Ask students to describe the mood of this painting. At what time of day does it take place? (Students can find both the moon and shadows.) Do any figures stand out more than others? Is the painting about a particular person or family, or a particular scene?
2. Ask students to compare the colors in this painting with those in paintings by either Matisse or Macke. How does the different use of colors contribute to different feelings in each work?
3. Ask students to talk about how the painting relates to the story.
4. Is it a busy or relaxing scene? Point out both the precise details in the buildings and the use of depth, or perspective. How do these techniques contribute to the setting?

Art Notes

"View of Nihonbashi Tori I-chome," by Utagawa Hiroshige (1797–1858)

Discussion suggestions:

1. Ask students what they think is going on beneath the big blue umbrella.
2. Point out how the painting has both many circular objects and straight lines. This makes the eye move over the figures, giving a dynamism (or motion) to the piece.
3. Ask students why no faces are shown. Have them compare this painting to the previous painting (p. 118) and also to Schlemmer's work (p. 40).

After You Read

Student Edition p. 122

What Do You Think? As an additional topic for discussion, students can compare the relationship of their parents or some other couple they know well with the relationship of the grandfather and grandmother in the story.

Student Edition p. 122

Activity Master 26

Try This: Story Mapping. Your students' story maps may vary from the following sample.

Use with student text pages 122, 186.

Story Map

TITLE: _Karate_	**AUTHOR:** _Huynh Quang Nhuong_
Story Elements:	
Characters:	The grandfather, the grandmother, the rascal, the restaurant owner, and the onlookers.
Setting:	A restaurant in Vietnam.
Initial Event:	A rascal insulted the grandfather.
Reaction:	Grandfather wanted to leave; grandmother made them stay and ignored the rascal. The rascal attacked the grandfather.
Goal-setting:	The grandmother decided to get rid of the rascal.
Attempt to reach goal:	The grandmother knocked the rascal over with her elbow. When he recovered and knocked over the table, she kicked him in the chin.
Outcomes:	The rascal collapsed. The grandmother, when asked where she learned karate, said her husband taught her.
Resolution:	Everyone respected the grandfather for his great knowledge of karate, and never bothered him again.

Technology Note: Enter the story map using the "tables" feature of a word processor. Have students then copy the file, fill in the cells, revise, edit, and print the final copy. They may wish to leave space for an illustration, or use the draw feature to illustrate.

Student Edition p. 123

Learning About Literature: Leads and Conclusions. Try one of the following suggestions to help students compare the leads and conclusions of stories (question 2). Ask students to choose a lead and conclusion from a selection in _Voices_ or from other short stories and novels that are available to your class.

1. Ask students to take turns reading leads, then discuss the class's reaction. Repeat the process with conclusions.

2. Assign half the class to read leads and half to read conclusions. Discuss after each reading.

3. Ask students to copy a lead on a strip of paper. Post all the strips. Give students three self-stick notes and tell them they can vote by putting the sticky notes on their favorite leads. Have them either put all their notes on one strip or divide them among the strips. Discuss the results of the voting and the reasons why the chosen lead is so effective.

Student Edition p. 123

Writing: Assist your students to become more proficient in the writing process by using some of the following suggestions.

1. **Prewriting:** Model the prewriting activity. Make a transparency of **Activity Master #26 (Story Map).** Model its use by filling in a family story from your experience.

2. **Drafting:** Emphasize to students that drafting is the time to get ideas down on paper. They should not worry about correctness of spelling and grammar yet.

3. **Sharing:** Ask students to use **Activity Master #6 (Conferring and Responding to Writing)** or teacher-made response forms.

4. **Revising:** Point out to students that revision is the time to add ideas, details, or information (based on peer and teacher input), to delete unnecessary details, and to organize the piece.

5. **Editing:** Ask students to use **Activity Master #14 (Editing Checklist).** Here are alternative ways to use the Editing Checklist:

   a) Have students check their own papers.
   b) Ask students to trade and edit papers in their response groups.
   c) Place all the student papers in a central location and ask students to edit as many papers as they can during class time. Have students either attach an editing checklist to the paper, or put the checklist in a separate stack to be distributed to the authors at the end of the class.

6. **Publication:** Help students to share their edited and polished family stories with other English or social studies classes.

▼ There Is No Word for Goodbye, by Mary TallMountain

Before You Read   **Student Edition p. 124**

Activity Master 27

Exploring Your Own Experience: How Do You Say Goodbye to Your Loved Ones?   Ask student groups to fill in ways of saying goodbye in as many languages as they know on **Activity Master #27.** Share with the students additional ways of saying goodbye.

Use with student text page 124.

How Do You Say Goodbye?

Way of saying goodbye	Language	English meaning
Goodbye	English	From "God be with you."
Aloha	Hawaiian	Word for both "hello" and "goodbye."
Ciao	Italian	"Hello" or "so long."
Adiós	Spanish	"To God."

After You Read

Student Edition p. 128

Activity Master 28

Try This: Marking the Poem. Distribute copies of **Activity Master #28** to students and ask them to mark copies as instructed in their text. If it is not possible to supply students with copies, ask them to use self-stick notes to mark the words and passages in their text, or to copy the poem by hand. Students' answers to the Activity will vary.

Student Edition p. 129

Learning About Literature: Imagery. Question 4: This poem communicates the high regard the Athlabaskans hold for their elderly people. The use of symbols from nature communicates their close connection to the natural world.

To promote intercultural communication, ask students to share the role elderly people play in their cultures. Have them also discuss the extent to which their cultures are connected to nature.

Student Edition p. 129

Writing: If possible, take the class on a field trip to a nearby park or an outdoor space on the school grounds and provide time for students to write their rough drafts. Alternately, the writing activity can be completed as homework.

Extension: Have students turn their narrative descriptions into poems. Ask them to focus on the strong images they have created. Those key phrases or images have the potential of becoming poems.

Before You Read

Student Edition p. 130

Activity Master 22

Exploring Your Own Experience: Round Table. Give each group one copy of **Activity Master #22 (Two-Column Chart).** Have students pass the chart around, with each person adding one idea to each column. To ensure that all students participate, ask them to use different color pens. At a glance, you can see if four colors have been used in rotation. Encourage students to use imagery. Students' charts will vary from the following sample.

ACTIVITY MASTER #22

Use with student text pages 82, 130, 134, 142.

Two-Column Chart (T-List)

Love is:	Love is not:
Giving	Selfish
Dancing all night	Playing Trivial Pursuit
Roses	Thistles
A sunny day	Cold rain
Walking in the park	Jogging
Talking on the phone	Waiting for a call
Listening	Yelling

Student Edition p. 132

Art Notes

"The Persistence of Memory," by Salvador Dali, 1931

Background:

Salvador Dali (1904–1989) was born in Catalonia, on the border of France and Spain. He painted dream imagery, showing everyday objects in unexpected forms. The inspiration for "The Persistence of Memory" was soft Camembert cheese! Dali, known for his flamboyance, published a book of humorous portraits of himself called *Dali's Mustache.*

Discussion suggestions:

1. Ask students to describe their reactions to the painting.
2. Have students talk about the way the painting relates to the poem. Which particular lines does it illustrate?
3. Ask students to guess why all the clocks are wilted. What does it mean? Why are there ants and flies on the clocks?
4. Ask students what they see in the central figure. A nose? An eyelash?

After You Read

Student Edition p. 134

Activity Master 22

Try This: Love is..., Love is not.... Remind students of the writing they did in the assignment for "There Is No Word for Goodbye" (Student Edition p. 129). They were asked to think of the five senses when writing descriptions. Suggest that they think again of the five senses when generating their T-lists for *Love is..., Love is not....* For example:

ACTIVITY MASTER #22

Use with student text pages 82, 130, 134, 142.

Two-Column Chart (T-List)

	Love is...	Love is not...
Sight:	Red roses in the garden	Thistles
Taste:	Tamales at Christmas	Stale bread
Hearing:	Temple bells	Thunder
Smell:	Perfumed air	Smoky rooms
Feel:	A warm jacket	A scratchy sweater

Student Edition p. 135

Activity Master 29

Writing: Feel free to tailor the **Responding to Poetry** form (**Activity Master #29**) to fit the level of your class as well as the subject matter of the poem. Asking students to respond in writing before eliciting oral feedback helps them become more proficient at responding thoughtfully and positively and gives them time to develop and formulate ideas. You can use the response forms to assess individual student's growth in giving thoughtful feedback.

Extension: Have students write poems expressing other emotions, for example, hate, embarrassment, sadness, or homesickness. Ask students to choose a topic, then group students who have chosen the same emotion. Using Round Table, the groups can generate metaphors for the emotion they have chosen. Then, have students write individual poems. Publish the poetry in a class book or submit it to a school newspaper or magazine.

▼ The Sullivan Ballou Love Letter, by Sullivan Ballou

Before You Read

Student Edition p. 136

Exploring Your Own Experience: Do a Quickwrite. Remind students that during a quickwrite their pens should not stop. If they are stuck, they can write, "I can't think of anything," or repeat the last line they have written until an idea comes to them.

Technology Note: Quickwrites can be done with a word processor. Turn the monitor off or the brightness down so the screen is blank. This will help students focus on their thoughts rather than the correctness of their writing.

Alternate Activity: Try this optional topic for the quickwrite: Ask students to describe an item they might choose to give someone as a symbol of love.

Background: Students may need additional background information on the Civil War and the events that led up to it. The following are some suggestions and resources:

- Students or their family members may have personal war experience that they could apply to a discussion of the Sullivan Ballou letter.
- Share with students the Civil War photographs by Matthew Brady.
- Show excerpts from Ken Burns's video series, *The Civil War*. Volume I has a moving reading of the letter, illustrated with original photographs and paintings of the war, and is accompanied by music of the time.

Reading the Letter: A variety of ways for helping students "through" the literature selections are provided in the Teacher's Guide, p. 21. Following is an additional suggestion. Read the letter aloud in class. Assign students to re-read the letter for homework. The next day, re-read the letter in class and discuss vocabulary and content.

Student Edition p. 138

Art Notes

"Trooper Meditating Beside a Grave," by Winslow Homer, 1865

Background:

Winslow Homer (1836–1910) was a self-taught naturalist painter who is considered one of the greatest American nineteenth-century artists. He made several trips to the front to draw and paint scenes from the American Civil War. His later paintings were influenced by his homes on the coasts of England and Maine.

Discussion suggestions:

1. Ask students to describe the colors of this painting. Are they warm or cold? Soft or bold?
2. Ask students whom they think the soldier is thinking about.
3. Point out how the trees' shadows fall to the left side, creating a sort of tall triangle shape like the man's. Why would Homer want to show a similarity between the man and nature in this picture?

After You Read

Student Edition p. 142

Activity Master 22

Try This: Charting Words. You may wish to have students work in pairs to fill out the chart for **Activity Master #22 (Two-Column Chart).** Your students' charts will vary from the following sample.

Two-Column Chart (T-List)
Sullivan Ballou's Two Loves

Country:	Family:
No misgivings about...the cause.	Love for you is deathless.
Willing to lay down my joys in this life to help maintain this government.	Bind me with mighty cables that nothing but Omnipotence could break.
Love of country comes over me like a strong wind.	Memories of blissful moments.
	Might have lived and loved together.
	Never forget how much I love you.
	I shall always be near you.

Extension: Found Poem. Ask students to write a "found" poem from the letter. Have them choose words or phrases from the letter, arrange them into poetic form, and give the poem a title.

Student Edition p. 143

Learning About Literature: For both *Conflict* and *Contrast,* use **Activity Master #22 (Two-Column Chart).** Your students' charts will vary from the following samples. If students need more support in completing both charts on conflict and on contrast, offer them one element and ask them to supply the conflicting or contrasting one.

Use with student text pages 82, 130, 134, 142.

Two-Column Chart (T-List)
Conflicts in Sullivan Ballou's Letter

Duty to country:	Duty to family:
Loves his country.	Loves Sarah.
Must give up hope for future.	Wants to live to see his sons grow up.
Must lay down the joys of this life.	Wants to live and love together with Sarah.
Knows death is final.	Hopes his spirit can visit Sarah.

Use with student text pages 82, 130, 134, 142.

Two-Column Chart (T-List)
Contrasts in Sullivan Ballou's Letter

Possibility of death by war:	Love that is deathless:
Nature as a strong wind taking men to war.	Nature as a soft breeze, a husband's breath upon his wife's cheek.
Feeling of despair that something will happen to him.	Feeling of hope in his son's prayer.
Gladdest days.	Darkest nights.
Relationship as many pains he had caused.	Relationship as many blissful moments.

Student Edition pp. 144–145

Activity Master 30

Writing: Writing a Letter.   If possible, coordinate the writing of historical letters with the social studies or history teacher.

Use **Activity Master #30 (Form for a Friendly Letter)** for the writing activity. Help students take their letters through the writing process using **Activity Master #14 (Editing Checklist)** for the final stage.

Have students share their letters with the class. Students who choose to write historical letters may want to share them with their social studies or history classes as well.

▼ **Balcony Scene from *West Side Story*, by Leonard Bernstein, Arthur Laurents, and Stephen Sondheim** _____

Before You Read   **Student Edition p. 146**

Activity Master 31

Exploring Your Own Experience: Ranking Ladder.   Use **Activity Master #31.** Model the ranking ladder activity on the chalkboard or overhead. Your students' ladders will vary from the following sample.

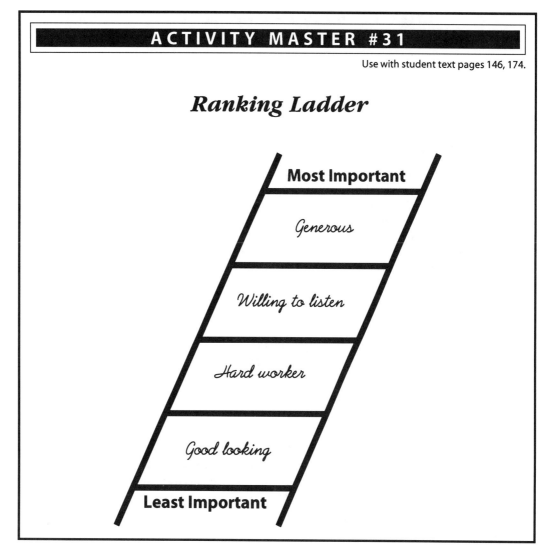

ACTIVITY MASTER #31

Use with student text pages 146, 174.

Ranking Ladder

Most Important

Generous

Willing to listen

Hard worker

Good looking

Least Important

Student Edition p. 146

Background. *Additional background suggestions:* Show a portion of the film, *West Side Story,* and/or play a recording of the song, "Tonight."

Reading the Selection: A variety of ways of helping students "through" the literary selections are listed in the Teacher's Guide, p. 21. The following are additional ideas:

- Have students perform dramatic readings of the scene in pairs.
- Read the scene aloud or have students read it.
- After students first practice quietly reading the scene, have them read it together, in chorus. Males can read Tony's role, and females can read Maria's.

Student Edition p. 152

Art Notes

Scene from the film *West Side Story*

Discussion suggestions:

1. Ask students to describe the scene. Is it crowded or spacious? Busy or calm?
2. Ask students how the feel of the plot might change if the photographer showed blue sky above the buildings.
3. How does this scene relate to issues in the play?

▼ Balcony Scene from *Romeo and Juliet,* by William Shakespeare ───────

Student Edition p. 156

Background: This selection is very challenging. We have included it at the request of teachers who want ESL students exposed to some selections that are frequently included in the regular high school curriculum. The following choices may help you and your students meet the challenge:

- Have students read only the portion of the scene that is included in the unit itself.
- Have students read the entire scene, both the portion in the unit and that in the Literary Appendix.
- Show students a video of act II, scene 2 from a stage or film version of the play.
- Play a recording of the dialogue from the scene.
- Paraphrase sections of the dialogue for students before they read.
- Read aloud a prose version of the story before reading the scene.
- Use a jigsaw activity. Form pairs of students and have each work on one portion of the dialogue to find the meaning of the words and paraphrase them so that they understand. Then have students share the meaning of their section with the class.
- Read the scene aloud dramatically.
- After an opportunity to practice, ask students to do a dramatic reading of the scene.

Student Edition p. 158

Art Notes

"Balcony Scene from *Romeo and Juliet,*" Stratford Theater, 1974

Discussion suggestions:

1. Ask students to compare this scene to that on p. 152
2. How do the two pictures illustrate different aspects of each play?

After You Read

Student Edition p. 164

Activity Master 23

Try This: Comparing and Contrasting Literature Using a Venn Diagram. Use **Activity Master #23** for this activity. Make an overhead transparency of the Venn Diagram. Fill in the information given in the diagram on p. 165 of the Student Edition. Ask students to find other details of setting to add to the diagram.

Hint: Write on a blank transparency of top of your Venn Diagram transparency to preserve it for future use.

Students' ideas for the Venn Diagram may vary from the following sample.

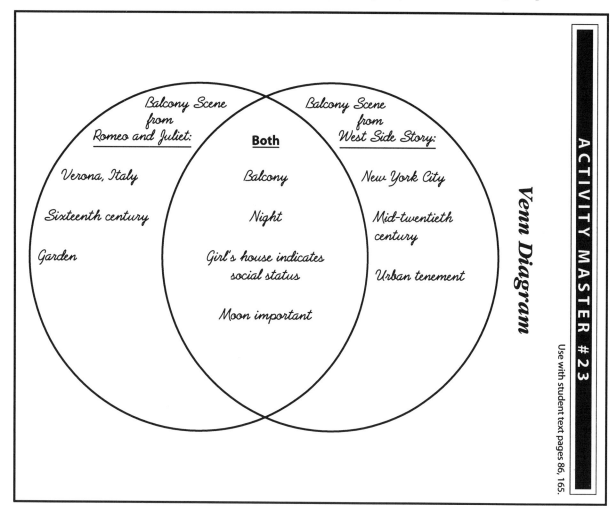

Venn Diagram

Balcony Scene from Romeo and Juliet:

Verona, Italy

Sixteenth century

Garden

Both

Balcony

Night

Girl's house indicates social status

Moon important

Balcony Scene from West Side Story:

New York City

Mid-twentieth century

Urban tenement

Group Work: Ask students to choose the element of the play they want to work on. Assign students who have chosen the same elements to work together. For example, students choosing "plot" would become one group. Groups should have no more than four members.

Have each group of students put their Venn Diagram on a transparency for class presentation.

Student Edition p. 165

Learning About Literature: Character Development. In preparation for a writing assignment, ask students to make a Venn Diagram comparing and contrasting two characters in the play. You may wish to have students work in pairs to put their Venn Diagrams on a large piece of paper and post the results. Students who choose to compare and contrast characters will have the classes' wealth of information as a resource. Students choosing setting will have the benefit of the group's sharing. Some students may choose a different element in the selection to compare and contrast, for example, plot.

Unit Follow-Up: Making Connections

Student Edition p. 167

Activity Master 32

Further Reading: Use **Activity Master #32** to help students find outside reading related to the unit. Before copying and distributing the Activity Master, add your own suggestions for further reading, and ask your students and your librarian for recommendations to add to the list.

Assessment Opportunities for Students in Unit 3: Love

See p. 40 of this Teacher's Guide for detailed suggestions.

1. Oral/Aural:

a) Tape students retelling a story—for example, the scene from *West Side Story* on pp. 147–154 of the Student Edition.

b) Have students record a portion of their discussion of *What Do You Think?* on p. 164. Ask them to summarize their discussion in a brief report. Record progress on the Oral/Aural Language Checklist.

2. Writing: Check the **Status of Writing Chart** (included in Appendix, p. 102) in the students' writing folders. Record student progress on the Writing Checklist.

3. Reading/Oral: Have students choose stories either from *Voices* or another source. Ask students to explain how the author reveals the characters in the story. Record student progress on the Reading Checklist. Ask students to make an oral report to the class and record student progress on the Oral/Aural Language Checklist.

4. Group Work: Observe students working together in writing response groups or in their *Think-Pair-Share* groups for "Karate." Have students self-evaluate their participation in the group using **Activity Master #15 (Group Project Evaluation).**

UNIT 4: ADVICE

Student Edition pp. 168–169

Art Notes

Unit Opener: "Morning," by Romare Bearden, 1979

Background:

Romare Bearden was born in his grandfather's house in Charlotte, North Carolina, in 1914. Growing up, Bearden would spend summers at his grandmother's boarding house in Pittsburgh, where many of his paintings are set. As an adult, Bearden joined many other African-American artists (painters, musicians, and writers) in Harlem, where he lived in an apartment over the Apollo Theatre. (This mass migration was later named the "Harlem Renaissance." Paul Dunbar, whose poem is on pp. 19–21, is also part of this artistic group.) Images of Bearden's community, especially the communities in the boarding houses of Pittsburgh, are important subjects in his works.

Discussion suggestions:

1. Ask students to describe their reactions to the colors in this work. What mood do they create?
2. How does the painting represent "advice"?
3. Ask students to look at the table in the center of the work. Why would Bearden want to put the fruit in the middle of the table instead of on top of it?
4. Why is this painting called "Morning"?

▼ Remember, by Joy Harjo

Before You Read

Student Edition p. 170

Exploring Your Own Experience: Remembering—Four Share. Ask a member of each group to record the things the group wants to remember on large piece of paper. Save these lists as a resource for students to use later in the writing activity (p. 175).

Extension: Homework/Categorizing

1. Instruct students to ask a parent or older member of their cultural community what they hope children will remember about their country and culture.
2. The next day, ask students to share the information they gathered.
3. Have a student record the ideas on the chalkboard or on chart paper to create a class list. The list might include:

   - Speak the language.
   - Respect people of all ages, especially elders.
   - Respect teachers.
   - Keep family ties strong.
   - Respect your grandparents and the sacrifices they made for you.
   - Keep the beliefs of your religion.

4. Ask students to suggest categories for organizing the ideas. They may generate such categories as people, beliefs, and appropriate behavior.
5. Make a chart as follows and save it as a resource for the writing activity (answers will vary).

People	Behavior	Beliefs
Grandparent who sacrificed	Speak language Respect people Respect teachers	Keep the religion

From the discussion, it should become clear to students that there are many ways to organize ideas into categories. You have modeled the process for them.

Reading the Poem: For the "We Wear the Mask" selection, this Teacher's Guide suggested "rendering" the poem aloud (p. 26). You may wish to use this technique again for this selection.

Student Edition p. 172

Art Notes

"Woman and Blueberries," by Patrick DesJarlait, 1972

Background:

Patrick DesJarlait (1921–1973), a Chippewa, was born in Red Lake, Minnesota. His paintings often depict figures working at common tasks. Although his images are softer and rounder than the cubists' flat square images, his work shows influences from that school. DesJarlait was also greatly influenced by Mexican muralists.

Discussion suggestions:

1. Have students compare this painting to Bearden's (p. 168). How are they alike or different in color or style?
2. Point out the symmetry of the two adult figures: we see each in profile, each has the same round shape, the trees add to the symmetry of DesJarlait's work as they frame the picture with round branches. See questions 1 and 3 for Manet's work (Unit 3 opener, pp. 110–111). Is DesJarlait's work more like Tamayo's or Manet's?

After You Read

Student Edition p. 174

What Do You Think? To save time, instruct students to write each of the things the poet wants the reader to remember (question 2) on a separate slip of paper. They will thus have completed step 2 for the Ranking Ladder activity.

Hint: Have students write on small self-stick notes.

Activity Master 31

Try This: Ranking Ladder. **Activity Master #31** is a graphic organizer used to help students list categories in order of importance. Students may create such categories as: heavenly bodies, people, nature, and life. Point out that there are many ways to group ideas into categories. Students' ranking ladders will vary from the following sample.

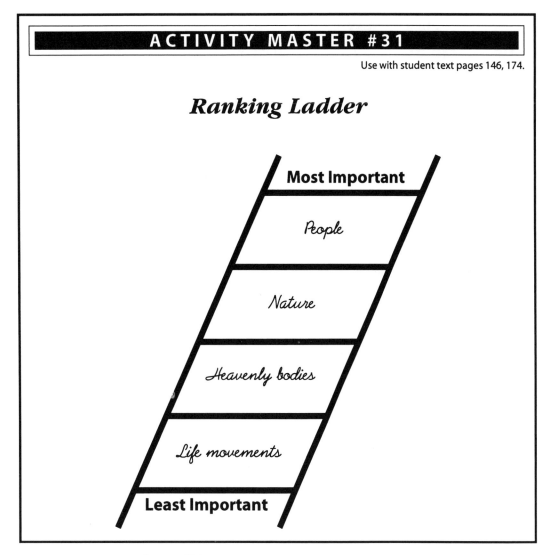

ACTIVITY MASTER #31

Use with student text pages 146, 174.

Ranking Ladder

Most Important

People

Nature

Heavenly bodies

Life movements

Least Important

Student Edition p. 175

Learning About Literature: Repetition. All the questions in this section about repetition help students discover that the poem is a chant that evokes the presence of things that should not be forgotten—almost as a litany or prayer. Emphasize this aspect of the exercise to your students.

Student Edition p. 175

Writing: Repetition. Remind students that the lists of ideas generated in the *Before You Read* activities will help stimulate their thinking about the poem they are to write. After students have completed rough drafts of their poems, have them meet in response groups. Use a response form similar to **Activity Master #29 (Responding to Poetry).**

▼ **Rules, by Karla Kushin** _____

Before You Read   **Student Edition p. 176**

Exploring Your Own Experience: Rules. Save the class list of rules that students generate, as they will need to refer to the list in *Try This*, Student Edition p. 180.

Art Notes

"Three Musicians," by Pablo Picasso, 1921

Background:

Pablo Picasso (1881-1973) is often considered the greatest painter of the twentieth century. The son of painter José Ruiz Blaso, Picasso took his mother's name. Although he was raised in Barcelona, Picasso settled in Paris, where he congregated with other painters like Henri Matisse, Juan Gris, and Georges Braque as well as important writers like Gertrude Stein. Picasso is perhaps best known for his contribution to cubism, a pictorial language that flattens shapes into two dimensions, and his mural, "Guernica" (1937), which was painted as a protest against fascism and war. Picasso believed that the artist should be as original as possible, as his statement to a friend suggests: "[An artist] should be very careful not to look for models. As soon as one artist takes another as a model, he is lost. There is no other point of departure than reality." Like all of his other "Three Musicians" paintings, this piece was originally life size.

Discussion suggestions:

1. Ask students if they like this painting. What images can they find in the piece? Point out the Harlequin figure. Tell students that many people described Picasso's painting as "fun." Ask them if they agree. Why?
2. Ask students if each one of these musicians has his or her own personality. What gives each an individual "style"?
3. Compare this work to Tamayo's painting on the cover of this book. How are the figures alike? Tell students that this style, which is called "cubism" shows three dimensional objects as they would appear after being squashed to two dimensions.

After You Read

Student Edition p. 180

What Do You Think? A variety of strategies for the *What Do You Think?* section are suggested on p. 18 of the Teacher's Guide. Here is another suggestion:

Inside Outside Circle. Ask students to stand and form two concentric circles. The inside circle faces out and the outside circle faces in so that each student faces a partner. Ask a question from *What Do You Think?* Set a time limit and instruct partners to discuss the question. Call time. Have students in the outside circle move ahead two persons. Pose the next question and continue the process until all the questions have been discussed.

Student Edition p. 180

Try This: Ironic or Metaphorical Advice. If needed, direct students to Student Edition Appendix B, *Guide to Literary Terms and Techniques,* to review verbal irony and metaphor.

Have students work in small groups to "jigsaw" Kuskin's rules. Assign each group three or four rules. Ask groups to brainstorm possible metaphorical meanings for the rules. Assign a student to record the group's work. Have groups share their favorite rule and metaphor with the class.

Activity Master 33

Model rewriting rules for students. Choose two or three of the rules students wrote in *Exploring Your Own Experience,* Student Edition p. 176. Students' rules may vary from the following sample.

Use with student text page 180.

Ironic or Metaphorical Advice

A. Write a list of rules for school, home, or life.

1. _Do not tease the cat._
2. _Do not leave without your umbrella._
3. _Always take the bus straight to school._
4. _Do not walk on the grass._
5. _____

B. Rewrite the rules with irony or metaphor.

> Hints: • Write the opposite.
> • Put the rule in an unusual setting.
> • Make the rule about an animal.

1. _Do not tease butterflies._
2. _Do not wear your umbrella in the house._
3. _Never ride a giraffe to school._
4. _Never walk on the cloud._
5. _____

C. Share and discuss your new rules with classmates. Choose one or more to edit and illustrate for a class book or display of rules.

> Rewritten rule:

> _____

> _____

If students are "stuck," suggest that they write a few rules they wish were true and turn them into negatives. For example, "Ride in a limo to school every day" might become "Never ride a limo to school." One further change would create "Never ride a giraffe to school."

Use **Activity Master #14 (Editing Checklist)** for the final step of the writing process.

Student Edition p. 181

Activity Master 34

Learning about Literature: Poetic Feet. Use the following suggestions to help students scan a poem:

1. Review the meter in "We Wear The Mask," Teacher's Guide p. 27 and "My moccasins have not walked," Teacher's Guide p. 32. Read a few lines from the poems. Ask students to use the eraser end of a pencil to gently tap the stressed syllables as you read.

2. Ask students to complete **Activity Master #34 (Poetic Rhythm).** You may wish to provide an audio cassette recording of the poem "Rules" to each group to help them hear the stressed and unstressed syllables.

Extension: Ask students to scan lines from the song "Tonight...Tonight!" from *West Side Story,* Student Edition p. 151, and from *Romeo and Juliet,* pp. 157-162. Use the jigsaw strategy if you like. Ask student pairs to put the scanned lines on an overhead, then explain to the class the kind of poetic foot the lines demonstrate.

Student Edition p. 181

Activity Master 14

Writing: Humorous Advice. Use **Activity Master #14 (Editing Checklist)** to help students edit their writing.

Extension 1: Ask other ESL classes or mainstream classes to write to your class for advice. Have students publish an advice newspaper and distribute it to all classes participating in the project.

Extension 2: Coordinate this activity with the social studies or history teacher. Ask students to write advice from a political or historical figure's point of view.

▼ A Mother's Advice, retold by Ahmed and Zane Zagbul _____

Before You Read

Student Edition p. 182

Activity Masters 9, 10, 8

Exploring Your Own Experience: Interviews—What Is a True Friend?
Remind students that they have many strategies for organizing information. Offer them a choice of the following strategies (with accompanying Activity Masters) to use in organizing the information they gathered in their interviews.

- **Activity Master #9 (Sunshine Outline),** Teacher's Guide p. 32

- **Activity Master #10 (Character Development Chart),** Teacher's Guide p. 35

- **Activity Master #8 (Cluster Chart),** Teacher's Guide p. 32

Extension: Students may enjoy making a class poem about friendship from the information gathered in the interviews.

Student Edition p. 184

Art Notes

"Arab Café," by Henri Matisse, 1913

Discussion suggestions:

1. Ask students to relate this painting to the story. How does its subject matter match? What about its mood or tone?

2. Have students compare this painting to Bearden's painting on Student Edition p. 168. Are the moods similar or different? Which pair of figures looks like better friends? Why?

3. Here is another painting where the faces of the figures are not seen. Ask students if they can still find a personality for each figure.

Student Edition p. 186

Activity Master 26

Try This: Story Map. Have students work in pairs to complete **Activity Master #26.** Remind students that they filled out a story map for "Karate" in Unit 3. Help those students who may need to review the "story elements."

Following is a story map of "A Mother's Advice." Your students' maps may vary from the following sample.

ACTIVITY MASTER #26

Use with student text pages 122, 186.

Story Map

TITLE: *A Mother's Advice*   **AUTHOR:** *Ahmed and Zane Zagbul*

Story Elements:	
Characters:	*Selim, Selim's mother, official's son, mayor's son, woodcutter's son.*
Setting:	*The countryside and the palace of an Egyptian Islamic Kingdom.*
Initial Event:	*Selim's mother advises him on the qualities of a true friend.*
Reaction:	
Goal-setting:	*Selim decides to find a true friend.*
Attempt to reach goal:	*Selim uses a test to find a true friend. He serves three eggs at breakfast to three "friends."*
Outcomes:	*The first two fail the test. The third, the woodcutter's son, passes the test.*
Resolution:	*Selim is a good friend to the woodcutter's son and makes him his number-one assistant.*

Technology Note: See Teacher's Guide p. 63 for using technology with a story map.

Learning About Literature: The Number Three In Folktales. Students may need a few days to gather folktales in which the number three appears. Have them ask family members, friends, or the school librarian to direct them to anthologies of fairy or folktales. Then, ask students in groups to retell their stories and fill out **Activity Master #35.** Have students from the same cultural background work together to fill out a chart for stories from their culture. Your students' charts will vary from the following sample.

ACTIVITY MASTER #35

Use with student text page 187.

The Number Three in Folktales

Folktale	Characters or Events That Come in Threes	Contrast or Extremes Shown
The Three Pigs	Three pigs built houses out of straw, sticks, bricks.	Two pigs took the easy way; one took the hard way and planned ahead. It was safest.
The Three Bears	Goldilocks visits the house of three bears.	The third chair, bed, and porridge were just right. The other two were extremes.
Tam Cam	An evil mother and daughter treat a stepdaughter badly.	Two characters are mean. The third is kind and honest, and is rewarded.
Little Burnt Face	Three daughters want to marry a warrior.	Two daughters lied. The third told the truth and married the warrior.

Student Edition pp. 187–188

Activity Master 36

Static and Dynamic Characters: Use **Activity Master #36** to determine which characters are static and which dynamic. Your students' answers may vary from the following sample.

Use with student text pages 187–188.

Are Characters Static or Dynamic?

Character	Description and actions at the beginning of the story	Description and actions at the end of the story	Dynamic (changed) or Static (stayed the same)
Lorena, in "The Raiders Jacket"	Lorena gets excited when Eddie loans her his jacket.	Lorena turns away from romance and buys practical gifts for her mom.	Dynamic
Rachel, in "Eleven"	Rachel wakes up on her 11th birthday and does not feel 11.	Rachel, worse than not feeling 11, wishes she was not 11.	Static
The Wise Woman, in "The Wise Woman of Córdoba"	Beautiful, clever, magic witch is put in jail.	Beautiful, clever, magic witch escapes from jail.	Dynamic

Note: Determining if Rachel in "Eleven," Student Edition pp. 11–14, is static or dynamic may be challenging to your students. You may need to remind them what a flashback is. Rachel is telling the story at the end of the school day, but flashes back to when she wakes up in the morning. The story chronologically begins when she wakes up.

Student Edition p. 189

Writing: Writing About Characterization. Have students use peer response groups to gain ideas for revision, and **Activity Master #14 (Editing Checklist)** to produce a polished piece.

▼ **Mother to Son, by Langston Hughes** ───────────────────

Before You Read

Student Edition p. 190

Activity Master 37

Exploring Your Own Experience: Ways of Speaking English. You may wish to assign the steps listed on p. 190 of the Student Edition as homework and group work as follows:

- **Steps 1 and 2:** *Homework.* Have students keep a journal of both the places they hear English and the kind of English they hear for 24 hours. Ask students to be specific. If they list their school, then they should note if it was in a classroom, hallway, cafeteria, office, or gym. If they hear English on television, then they should note if it was a news broadcast, situation comedy, or game show. They also need to be aware of who is speaking to whom. In the classroom, they should note if the teacher is talking to students, or students are talking to each other or the teacher.

- **Steps 3–5:** *Group Work.* The next day in class, have students work together in groups to create a chart from their notes. Display the charts.

Background: Students may be confused by the fact that Hughes is using a mother's voice in the poem. The point of view of the poem does not have to be the poet's point of view. Review **point of view,** and focus on the title of the poem before reading.

Student Edition pp. 191–193

You may wish to use the suggestions for "rendering," Teacher's Guide p. 26.

Student Edition p. 192

Art Notes

"Woman in Calico," by William H. Johnson, 1944

Background:

William H. Johnson (1901–1970), who is both African-American and part Sioux, was born and raised in Florence, South Carolina. He later studied in France and traveled through Denmark and Norway. He continued to travel between the United States and Scandinavia throughout his life, as he married a woman from Denmark. His work draws heavily upon his childhood in South Carolina and is known for a primitive expression of black culture.

Discussion suggestions:

1. Ask students to describe their reaction to this painting. What is this woman like in "real" life? Old or young? Nice or mean?
2. Does this figure look like other figures in the book? Why? How is this painting different from Frida Kahlo's portrait on p. 76? Which one of the women looks richer? Nicer?
3. Ask students to explain why they can see only one half of the chair. Why does the artist use two different backdrops? Have them cover up one side of the painting and then the other. Does the woman look different on each side?

After You Read

Student Edition p. 194

Learning About Literature: Analogy

Extension: Pair Work. Have students illustrate the metaphors in the poem on one half of a piece of paper. On the other half, have them write an analogous life situation. Students can choose the person whose life they wish to draw an analogy to from the mother in the poem, one of their own family members, or a person they know well. For example, stairs with boards torn up might be accompanied by the life analogy "My father was gone for a year looking for work."

Gallery Tour: Post student work and have students tour this "gallery" of work. Have them make notes in their journals of analogies they find interesting.

Student Edition p. 195

Writing: Using Analogies. Encourage students to use a prewriting strategy such as clustering **(Activity Master #8)** to brainstorm ideas before writing. If students get good results, they might want to transform their paragraphs into poems.

▼ Conceit, by Elizabeth Ruiz

Before You Read

Student Edition p. 196

Activity Master 38

Exploring Your Own Experience: Proverbs. If your class includes several students from particular language groups, you may wish to have them work together in home language groups to make an illustrated chart of proverbs in their language accompanied by the English meaning. Post the results for students to learn from and to enjoy proverbs from other cultures.

Homework: Assign students the task of collecting several proverbs or sayings in English. These will be used as a resource in *Try This,* Student Edition p. 198.

Student Edition p. 197

Art Notes

"Reflection," by G.G. Kopilak, 1979

Background:

G.G. Kopilak is an artist now living in New York. Kopilak was trained in Italy and New York.

Discussion suggestions:

1. Have students compare this painting to the photograph on p. 34. How are they alike? Different?
2. The woman in the painting by Kopilak is looking both through a window (stained glass) and at her reflection. Is she looking outside or at herself?
3. How does this painting illustrate the poem?

After You Read

Student Edition p. 199

Writing: Using Proverbs. Remind students that they know several strategies to help them through the steps of the writing process. For example, for **prewriting,** they may want to "cluster" a proverb by drawing a circle around it and writing as many ideas associated with it as they can think of. Perhaps the ideas will bring another proverb to mind. The cluster can become the basis for a poem or short story. Have students work with their response groups to **revise** their writing. They can use **Activity Master #6 (Conferring and Responding to Writing)** to assist them in giving one another helpful positive feedback.

Extension: If you have a good collection of proverbs in students' native languages and translations, you might publish a book of proverbs from many countries to share with social studies or other classes.

▼ *La Peseta* (The Quarter), from *Stories from El Barrio,* by Piri Thomas _____

Before You Read

Student Edition p. 200

Background: You may wish to supply your students with more information on the Great Depression. If possible, coordinate with the social studies or history teacher.

Reading the Poem: We believe that reading is the process of constructing meaning by interacting with text. Assist your students in becoming more proficient and reflective readers by asking them to use **marginalia,** that is, recording their thought processes as they read. Ask them to raise questions, offer opinions, make connections to life experiences, appreciate style, or predict. Have students record their thoughts as they read in a wide margin next to the text. If you choose to use marginalia, here are some suggestions:

1. Have students post self-stick notes next to each stanza in the textbook.
2. Model the process using the first stanza or two. After reading the first stanza, you might express thoughts similar to these:

   - "He uses Spanish words. That helps me see him as a person from a Spanish-speaking country."
   - "I see a boy in brown baggy pants standing outside a dirty candy store window."
   - "I wonder if he really stole a candy bar. That bothers me because it is wrong. If he did, he probably never got caught."
   - "I like the way the author talks to me. He said, 'You know,....'"

3. If you choose to read the poem aloud, pause after each stanza or two, allowing students time to record their thoughts.

4. When you have finished reading the poem, ask volunteers to share some of their thoughts.

Student Edition p. 202

Art Notes

"Construction of a Dam" (Mural study, Department of the Interior), by William Gropper, 1937

Background:

William Gropper, the son of impoverished Jewish immigrants, was born in 1897 in New York City. His work is characterized as Social Realism, which means that he often represented displaced and oppressed persons or classes in a blunt and graphic way. Because of his increasingly liberal politics, Gropper was asked to testify before congress during Joseph McCarthy's anti-communist campaign. This experience apparently did not damage Gropper's career, as he gained renewed popularity during the 1960s.

Discussion suggestions:

1. Ask students to describe the setting of this painting. What time of day is it? How hot is it? Then have them describe the colors. Are they warm, or cold? How do the colors add to the way they feel about the workers?

2. Point out how the workers are concentrated in one corner of the painting. What effect does this have? (A sense of intensity to the work, a sense of being crowded?)

Student Edition p. 206

Art Notes

"Boy in Blue *(Niño en azul),*" by Rufino Tamayo, 1928

Discussion suggestions

1. Ask students to describe the colors. Are they bold and exciting? Or flat and soft? What mood do the colors create? How does the mood relate to the poem? Why is this painting called "Boy in Blue" when the boy is dressed in khaki?

2. What other paintings does this work resemble? How does it compare to a painting by Matisse? How is it similar to or different from Johnson's on p. 192?

3. What is the expression on the boy's face? Does it seem appropriate to the story?

After You Read

Student Edition p. 210

What Do You Think? Question Pairs. Prior to asking the *What Do You Think?* questions, you might try **question pairs.** If students have used marginalia successfully, ask student pairs to use their notes to formulate questions about the poem. Then ask the pairs to exchange questions with another pair. After questions are answered, the answers are returned for correction to the pair who originally wrote the question.

Try This: Idioms. *Homework:* Students will need a day or two to collect the idioms they need in this activity.

Technology Note: Have students use the word processor to keep a personal list of idioms they want to remember. They can use the line or paragraph sort feature to alphabetize their lists, then print the files for inclusion in their notebooks. Once they are confident that they know the idioms well, they can delete them from the file.

Student Edition p. 211

Activity Master 39

Learning About Literature: Narrative and Lyric Poems. Point out to students that some poems bridge the two categories of narrative and lyric. "Conceit" has elements of a lyric poem but could also be considered a narrative poem because it tells a story. Use **Activity Master #39.** Your students' charts will vary from the following sample.

Use with student text page 211.

Narrative and Lyric Poetry

Title	Narrative or Lyric?
La Peseta	narrative
My moccasins have not walked	lyric
We Wear the Mask	lyric
Ode to My Socks	lyric
hist whist	lyric
The Raven	narrative
Although I Conquer All the Earth	lyric
There is No Word for Goodbye	lyric
Solo for Saturday Night Guitar	lyric
Remember	lyric
Rules	lyric
Mother to Son	lyric/narrative
Conceit	lyric/narrative

Student Edition p. 211

Writing: Lessons from Childhood. *Prewriting Activity:* Model this activity before asking students to try it. Draw a map of an area where you lived as a child. It might be a neighborhood or a plan of a house. Label the drawing with key phrases brought to mind of events that happened there, then choose the incident you wish to write about.

Have students draw and label their own maps and chose an event to write about. Students may use **Activity Master #9 (Sunshine Outline)** or **Activity Master #26 (Story Map)** to outline the elements of their stories.

Before You Read

Student Edition p. 212

Exploring Your Own Experience: Round Table. Before the Round Table discussion, model by telling students some things that you do well. Give students a few moments to think of what they do well that they want to share in the Round Table discussion.

Note: To promote intercultural understanding and communication, ask students to discuss from the point of view of their culture both the appropriateness and method used of talking about what one does well.

Technology Note: Have students sit around a computer and in turn type in things they do well. Then have them print the results to post in the classroom.

Student Edition p. 212

Background: You may want to have students see the video *Searching for Bobby Fisher,* which tells the story of a young chess player.

Reading the Selection: Ask students to record their thinking processes while they read by using marginalia (see Teacher's Guide p. 85). Ask them to use marginalia for either all or a portion of the story.

Student Edition p. 216

Art Notes

"Ladies Playing Double Sixes," Style of Chou Fang. China, Song dynasty, 10th/11th century

Background:

Chou Fang (Sung dynasty, 10th–11th century) is known for painting plump palace ladies. These ladies are playing double-sixes, which is a game similar to backgammon.

Discussion suggestions:

1. Ask students to describe the mood of this painting. Is it serious or fun?
2. What are the women in the upper left doing? Does their presence say anything about the importance of this game?

After You Read

Student Edition p. 220

Activity Master 40

Try This: The Best Game Debate. If multiple cassette recorders are not available, you can use one audio cassette recorder to record one group's discussion and play a portion of it for the whole class to transcribe.

Extension: Ask students to teach a favorite game from their country to the rest of the class. Groups of students from the same country may want to work together to develop written instructions before teaching the game, or students in the class can write the instructions after the game has been demonstrated to them.

Student Edition p. 221

Learning About Literature: Dialogue

Extension: Discuss what dialogue is and have students point to an example in "Four Directions." Ask students to find an example of the use of dialogue in another story from *Voices Gold.* Then divide students into groups of four to have a Round Table discussion (Student Edition p. 98). Have students, in turn, tell the group the title of the story, the name of the character speaking, and the page number of the example. Then have the student read the dialogue and explain why he or she likes the way the author has written that piece of dialogue. For easy reference, have a recorder in the group write the character names and page numbers where the selection was found. Finally, have each group choose one example of dialogue to share with the class.

Writing: A Short Story with Dialogue. For this writing assignment, have three Activity Masters available for students: **Activity Master #40 (Writing People's Speech)**, **Activity Master #26 (Story Map)**, and **Activity Master #21 (Character Web)**.

Extension: Ask students to apply what they have learned about the use of dialogue as a means of "showing," not just "telling." Ask them to look through their writing folders to find a story they want to revise by including dialogue.

▼ On the Pulse of Morning (excerpt), by Maya Angelou

Before You Read

Student Edition p. 222

Exploring Your Own Experience: Tree of Hope. When the "Tree of Hope" is finished and on display, you might want to create a class poem. Each hope from the tree could become a line in the poem.

Background: "On the Pulse of Morning" is the final piece of literature in *Voices Gold* because we wanted to end the book with inspiring and uplifting words. The poem is a stirring message of hope for positive change. It is a patriotic plea for respect for all people, past and present. You may wish to share with your students the honor it was for Maya Angelou to be chosen to write a poem for the presidential inauguration of William Jefferson Clinton.

Student Edition p. 224

Art Notes

"Men Exist for the Sake of One Another. Teach Them Then or Bear With Them," by Jacob Lawrence, 1958

Background:

Jacob Lawrence was born in Atlantic City, New Jersey, in 1917. He moved with his mother to Harlem. While in his 20s, Lawrence was the first black artist to have a one-man show at the Museum of Modern Art in New York City. Lawrence's work primarily takes African-American experience as its subject matter; stylistically, it is known for its combination of realism with abstract design.

Discussion suggestions:

1. What are the children and the man doing?
2. Ask students to guess why a tree grows from the man's hand.
3. Ask students how the painting relates to the poem. Ask them how the tone of the poem and the bright colors are related. Also, see if they find particular images in both the painting and the poem.

After You Read

Student Edition p. 227

What Do You Think? You may want to review "symbol" with the students. Direct them to the definition for symbol in the *Guide to Literary Terms and Techniques*, Student Edition p. 242. Ask students to brainstorm other symbols.

Try This: Revising for Powerful Verbs

Technology Note: Students can use the "search and replace" function of a word processor to find forms of the verb "to be." They can use the thesaurus feature to find stronger verbs to fit in their place.

Extension: Have students express their understanding of the poem through art using one of these suggestions:

1. Have students illustrate a favorite phrase or line that offers advice. Ask them to draw a picture incorporating the line or phrase from the poem or draw a picture captioned by the line.
2. Have students make a collage to represent an important message they found in the poem. Have them use pictures cut out of magazines combined with their own drawings. Then have them explain their collages to a group of students.

Unit Follow-Up: Making Connections

Student Edition p. 228

Activity Master 41

Advice Chart: Use **Activity Master #41** with Unit Follow-Up suggestion 3, Student Edition p. 228. Make a transparency of the chart to help you explain the activity and demonstrate how to get started. Your students' charts may vary from the following sample.

ACTIVITY MASTER #41

Use with student text page 228.

Advice in Unit 4

Title	Person Offering Advice	Advice
Remember	Wise person	Remember your place in the universe and your roots.
Rules	An adult	Rules don't have to be serious, but they are important.
A Mother's Advice	Mother	Choose a friend carefully to be sure he or she is a true friend.
Conceit	Woman or Ruiz	What is inside a person is more important than beauty.
La Peseta	Father	Honesty is always the best policy.
Four Directions	Mother or Amy Tan	A mother's confidence and advice are important for children to succeed.
On the Pulse of Morning	Maya Angelou	Have hope in the future and trust your country and fellow human beings.

Student Edition p. 229

Activity Master 42

Further Reading: Use **Activity Master #42** to help students find outside reading related to the unit. Before copying and distributing the Activity Master, add your own suggestions for further reading, and ask your students and your librarian for recommendations to add to the list.

Assessment Opportunities for Students in Unit 4: Advice

See p. 40 of this Teacher's Guide for detailed suggestions.

1. **Aural/Oral/Writing:**

   a) Have students tape a portion of *What Do You Think?* Ask them to transcribe the discussion using the rules for quotation marks p. 221 of the Student Edition. Have them record their progress on item 7 of the Aural/Oral Checklist. Students can trade papers to evaluate correct usage of quotation marks.

   b) Have students select and tape a passage to

   • read aloud
   • retell in their own words

   c) Have students review their audio or video tape for the year. Ask them to record their growth based on the criteria you or they have set for the class.

2. **Writing:** Ask students to work with you in preparing their final portfolios. The pieces of writing students select should show growth in understanding the writing process, in mastery of writing skills, and in understanding elements of literature. Portfolios can include:

   • examples from all the stages of writing
   • checklists
   • feedback from teacher and peers
   • best piece(s) and an explanation of why it is "best"
   • a piece they would like to improve and how they would improve it
   • areas for improvement they would like to work on in the future.

3. **Reading:** Ask students to record in their reading logs marginalia on a story they have read outside class. Record growth on the Reading Checklist.

4. **Best Game Debate:** Have students assess individual and group process during a discussion such as The Best Game Debate, Student Edition p. 220.

5. **Student Self-Evaluation:** Encourage students to use Unit Project Idea 7 (Student Edition p. 229) to assess what they have learned from *Voices Gold* and what they would like to learn next about literature. You might choose to use a transparency of a two-column chart with columns labeled "Learned" and "Want to Learn." Fill out the chart as a group activity, then have each individual write his or her own paragraph.

TEACHER RESOURCES FOR
VOICES IN LITERATURE

Allen, V. (1989). Literature as a support to language acquisition. In P. Rigg & V. Allen (Eds.). *When they don't all speak English: Integrating the ESL student into the regular classroom.* Urbana, IL: National Council of Teachers of English.

Atwell, N. (1987). *In the middle: Writing, reading and learning with adolescents.* Portsmouth, NH: Heinemann.

Atwell, N. (Ed.). (1990). *Coming to know: Writing to learn in the intermediate grades.* Portsmouth, NH: Heinemann.

Bell, J. (1991). *Teaching multilevel classes in ESL.* San Diego, CA: Dominie Press.

Bellanca, J. (1990). *The cooperative think tank: Practical techniques to teach thinking in the cooperative classroom.* Palatine, IL: Skylight Publishing.

Bishop, R.S. (1987). Extending multicultural understanding through children's books. In B.E. Cullinan (Ed.). *Children's literature in the reading program.* Newark, DE: International Reading Association, 60-67.

Blair, L. (1991). Developing student voices with multicultural literature. *English Journal, 80*:8, 24-28.

California Department of Education. (1988, 1990). *Recommended readings in literature, K-8 and addendum.* Sacramento, CA: California State Department of Education.

California Department of Education. (1990). *Recommended literature, 9-12.* Sacramento, CA: California State Department of Education.

California Literature Institute. (1985). *Literature for all students: A sourcebook for teachers.* Sacramento, CA: California State Department of Education.

Calkins, L. (1986). *The art of teaching writing.* Portsmouth, NH: Heinemann.

Collie, J. & Slater, S. (1987). *Literature in the language classroom: A resource book of ideas and activities.* New York: Cambridge University Press.

Cox, S. & Galda, L. (1990). Multicultural literature: Mirrors and windows on a global community. *The Reading Teacher, 43,* 582-589.

Day, R.R. (1993). *New ways in teaching reading.* Alexandria, VA: TESOL.

Elley, W.B. & Mangubhai, F. (1983). The impact of reading on second language learning. *Reading Research Quarterly, 19,* 53-67.

Enright, D.S. & McCloskey, M.L. (1988). *Integrating English.* Reading, MA: Addison-Wesley.

Frank, M. (1979). *If you're trying to teach kids how to write, you've gotta have this book.* Nashville, TN: Incentive Publications.

Freeman, Y. & Freeman, D. (1989). A road to success for language-minority high school students. In P. Rigg & V. Allen (Eds.). *When they don't all speak English: Integrating the ESL student into the regular classroom.* Urbana, IL: National Council of Teachers of English.

Freeman, Y. & Freeman, D. (1989). Whole language approaches to writing with secondary students of English as a second language. In D. Johnson & D. Roen (Eds.). *Richness in writing: Empowering ESL students.* New York: Longman.

Freeman, Y. & Freeman, D. (1992). *Whole language for second language learners.* Portsmouth, NH: Heinemann.

Gajdusek, L. (1988). Toward a wider use of literature in ESL: Why and how. *TESOL Quarterly, 22,* 227-257.

Goodman, K.S., Goodman, Y.M. & Hood, W.J. (Eds.). (1988). *The whole language evaluation book.* Portsmouth, NH: Heinemann.

Graves, D. (1983). *Writing: Teachers and children at work.* Portsmouth, NH: Heinemann.

Graves, D. & Sunstein, B.S. (Eds.). (1992). *Portfolio portraits.* Portsmouth, NH: Heinemann.

Hayes, C., Bahruth, R. & Kessler, C. (1991). *Literacy con cariño.* Portsmouth, NH: Heinemann.

Heath, S.B. & Mangiola, L. (1991). *Children of promise: Literate activity in linguistically and culturally diverse classrooms.* Washington DC: National Education Association.

Hickman, J. & Cullinan, B. (1989). *Children's literature in the classroom: Weaving Charlotte's Web.* Needham Heights, MA: Christopher-Gordon Publishers.

Holt, D.D. (1993). *Cooperative learning: A response to linguistic and cultural diversity.* McHenry, IL: Delta Systems and The Center for Applied Linguistics.

Hudelson, S. (1989). *Write on: Children writing in ESL.* Englewood Cliffs, NJ: Center for Applied Linguistics and Prentice Hall Regents.

Johnson, Y. & Louis, D. (1987). *Literacy through literature.* Portsmouth, NH: Heinemann.

Koch, K. (1970). *Wishes, lies, and dreams: Teaching children to write poetry.* New York: Vintage.

Koch, K. & Farrell, K. (1982). *Sleeping on the wing: An anthology of modern poetry with essays on reading and writing.* New York: Vintage.

Langer, J.A. (1991). *Literary understanding and literature instruction.* Repr. 2.11. Albany, NY: Center for the Learning and Teaching of Literature.

Lu, J.H. (1989). *A resource guide for Asian and Pacific American students, K–12.* Oakland, CA: National Association for Asian and Pacific American Education.

Murray, D.E. (1992). *Diversity as resource: Redefining cultural literacy.* Alexandria, VA: TESOL.

Peitzman, F. & Gadda, G. (1991). *With different eyes: Insights into teaching language minority students across the disciplines.* Los Angeles, CA: UCLA Center for Academic Interinstitutional Programs.

Peterson, R. & Peterson, M. (Eds.). (1990). *Grand conversations: Literature groups in action.* Ontario, Canada: Scholastic.

Peyton, J.K. & Reed, L. (1990). *Dialogue journal writing with nonnative English speakers: A handbook for teachers.* Alexandria, VA: TESOL.

Schon, I. (1978). *Hispanic heritage: A guide to juvenile books about Hispanic people and cultures,* Series 1–4. Metuchen, NJ: Scarecrow Press, 1980–91.

Short, K. & Pierce, K. (1990). *Talking about books.* Portsmouth, NH: Heinemann.

Slapin, B., Seale, D. & Gonzales, R. (1988). *How to tell the difference: A checklist for evaluating Native American children's books.* Berkeley, CA: Oyate.

Smallwood, B.A. (1990). *The literature connection: A read-aloud guide for multicultural classrooms.* Reading, MA: Addison-Wesley.

Taylor, P. (Ed.). (1989). *From literacy to literature: Reading and writing for the language minority student—A sourcebook for teachers.* Los Angeles, CA: UCLA Center for Academic Interinstitutional Programs.

Tharp, R.G. & Gallimore, R. (1991). *Rousing minds to life.* New York: Cambridge University Press.

APPENDIX

**CHECKLISTS FOR USE
IN STUDENT ASSESSMENT
IN CONJUNCTION WITH
*VOICES IN LITERATURE***

Oral/Aural Language Checklist

Student's Name

Codes: **C** = in control **D** = developing **NY** = not yet

Assessment Item	Beginning of Year Date:		Middle of Year Date:		End of Year Date:	
	Code	Comments	Code	Comments	Code	Comments
1. Reports and describes things he or she wants, does. Makes simple requests.						
2. Tells a story (real or imaginary) with a sequence of events.						
3. Takes notes from classroom instructions/ descriptions/ presentations.						
4. Successfully plans, conducts, and reports on interview with stranger.						
5. Makes clear and comprehensible oral presentation before class.						
6. Interprets literature (poem, drama, or prose) in clear presentation.						
7. Participates in literary discussion.						
Teacher notes:						

Reading Checklist

Student's Name

Record your observations of the student's English reading skills and behaviors on this assessment checklist. Note the date and make specific comments about the situations and behaviors you observe.

Assessment Item	Beginning of Year	Middle of Year	End of Year
Participates in shared reading. Chants portions of the text, supplies missing words.			
Makes predictions about story events. Participates in discussions and dramatization of poems and stories.			
Enjoys books independently and discusses with peers. Number of books read independently this term/period:			
Offers interpretation of literary elements of setting, plot, and theme.			
Retells story in own words.			
Successfully outlines story elements on story map.			
Successfully obtains meaning from print. Note length and difficulty of passage, or include sample.			
Recognizes and explains the use of poetic elements and devices—simile, metaphor, rhyme, rhythm—appealing to the senses.			

Teacher comments/notes:

Writing Checklist

Student's Name

Codes: C = in control   D = developing   NY = not yet

Grade: Mo./Yr.							Assessment Item and Comments
							Student dictates ideas.
							Student writes captions and full name.
							Student writes to a variety of audiences: self, trusted adult, teacher as partner in dialogue, and known and unknown audiences.
							Student expresses ideas in complete thoughts.
							Student writes recognizable paragraphs.
							Student writes paragraphs with indentation, topic sentence, details, or supportive and concluding sentences.
							Student explores several genres of writing using the writing process, e.g., poetry, personal narrative, nonfiction, fiction, persuasive writing, and speeches.

Student Self-Assessment Form*

My Progress in ESOL

Name   Teacher

Grade   Date

Part 1: Please circle the number that best describes you:

How I feel about my work in ESOL this week:

Happy	1	2	3	4	*Unhappy*

My speaking and listening are:

Improving	1	2	3	4	*Not improving*

My reading is:

Improving	1	2	3	4	*Not improving*

My writing is:

Improving	1	2	3	4	*Not improving*

My work is:

Too easy	1	2	3	4	*Too hard*

My work is:

Very interesting	1	2	3	4	*Not interesting*

Part 2: Please finish the sentences.
(You can write more on the back of this page if you want to.)

The best thing I did/learned lately is

I would like to learn

New places I am using English now are

I am best at

I need some help with

My learning and practicing plans are to

*Students may use this form periodically to assess their own progress.

Status of Writing Chart

Student's Name

Title of Piece	Prewriting	Draft	Peer Conference	Revision	Editing Conference w/Teacher	Publication
	(DATE)	(DATE)	(DATE)	(DATE)	(DATE)	(DATE)
	Comments:					
	(DATE)	(DATE)	(DATE)	(DATE)	(DATE)	(DATE)
	Comments:					
	(DATE)	(DATE)	(DATE)	(DATE)	(DATE)	(DATE)
	Comments:					
	(DATE)	(DATE)	(DATE)	(DATE)	(DATE)	(DATE)
	Comments:					
	(DATE)	(DATE)	(DATE)	(DATE)	(DATE)	(DATE)
	Comments:					
	(DATE)	(DATE)	(DATE)	(DATE)	(DATE)	(DATE)
	Comments:					